Variable
Valve
Timings

Variable Valve Timings

MEMOIRS OF A CAR TRAGIC

CHRIS HARRIS

EBURY
SPOTLIGHT

1

Ebury Spotlight, an imprint of Ebury Publishing
20 Vauxhall Bridge Road
London SW1V 2SA

Ebury Spotlight is part of the Penguin Random House group of companies
whose addresses can be found at global.penguinrandomhouse.com

Penguin
Random House
UK

First published by Ebury Spotlight in 2023

www.penguin.co.uk

A CIP catalogue record for this book is available from the British Library

All pictures within the book from Chris Harris's private collection.

ISBN 9781529913590

Printed and bound in Great Britain by TJ Books Ltd, Padstow, Cornwall

The authorised representative in the EEA is Penguin Random House
Ireland, Morrison Chambers, 32 Nassau Street, Dublin D02 YH68

Penguin Random House is committed to a sustainable future for
our business, our readers and our planet. This book is made
from Forest Stewardship Council® certified paper.

To C, X, H

CONTENTS

ONE
TOY CARS

It always begins with a toy car. Or at least it always began with a toy car – nowadays it's probably a tweet or a TikTok or something virtual. But if you're someone of an age who can even vaguely relate to what this 48-year-old man is typing, then I reckon it started with a toy car.

There is something binary about the way young people respond to the form of a motor car, whether it's on television, in the raw or a scale model. Children point and whoop at exciting-looking machinery because they are uninhibited by the societal baggage that the motor car carries for many adults in 2023. Nothing makes me smile inside more than seeing a kid want to stop and ogle at a low-slung slice of Italian machinery, as their appalled parent tries to drag them away while delivering a sermon on the evils of the motor car. What a sad, joyless life they must lead. I bet they didn't love toy cars when they were young.

CHAPTER ONE

I still have the box of toy cars that was the centre of my universe at around the time my first memories began to form. They are quite unremarkable and show no signs of having been curated to satisfy an enthusiasm for any particular type or shape. They are also in terrible condition, which must confirm that behavioural traits manifest themselves early in life because I still don't look after my things – especially motor cars. In fact, I take impish satisfaction in knowing that those around me are appalled by how dirty and unloved my motor cars look. Mechanically, they are fit as a whippet, but the aesthetic has never interested me in the least. There are events for people who polish cars – actual celebrations of people who have specific methods of washing and polishing cars, and they award each other medals and money for the static preparation of an object designed to move. How perverse is that? The only beautiful static car is one that has just been driven hard and is caked in the dirt and insects that describe the journey it just completed. Better still, a racing car that has just won, not been washed and parked in a museum. That I can understand. But not polishing for the sake of polishing.

But those early toy cars were so precious. If you're a car person – and I have to assume that if you're reading this, you are – you might have reflected on your formative years and drawn the same conclusion. And that is this: the level of protection and obsession you felt towards those little Majorette and Corgi toys was a brief prologue to your later life. It certainly was for me. I don't have a very good memory (which isn't ideal for the purposes of writing a book) but I do remember things that involved cars, so my first memory does just that.

It involves my late mother and a beach, and a bucket of toy cars. She told me many years ago that she left me playing with them and when the time came to pack up and head back, there was a problem. I'd buried the cars but couldn't quite remember where. This bit I don't remember at all, nor the next scene which involved my poor mother digging up a large section of beach looking – and failing – to find four tiny, dented lumps of metal that could easily be replaced. Parents really are wonderful, patient things.

The part I do remember is the aftermath, the feeling of utter desolation in the hotel room because my precious friends (because that's what they were, they weren't just inanimate objects – we had adventures together) had gone. They were the pals from the fantasy life so many kids hide in because they have no siblings, or maybe just retreat to because it's safe and fun. Now that I make television I have a therapist, because it's part of the uniform. When we discussed bereavement, I told him my first experience of emotional loss was my grandmother on my mother's side. But it wasn't at all – it was those toy cars. I was desperately sad to lose them because they mattered to me on so many levels. I must have tried not to cry but probably did weep buckets. I was a terrible crier as a child and have become a terrible non-crier as an adult. The irony is that I wasn't remotely upset when that grandmother passed away. She was a hideous old boot and not a patch on a Majorette Renault 14.

CHAPTER ONE

The next time this happened was a true test of emotional allegiance. If toy cars were my world, my dog Toby probably constituted the rest of it. You can probably guess where this is going. Toby thought my precious 1982 Williams FW07B Scalextric car was even more delicious than I did, so when we were at church one Sunday he ate a good portion of it. I was beside myself and, to teach me the lesson of not leaving stuff lying around, the Williams wasn't replaced. Later in life I realised that Toby was merely choosing an extreme form of protest to stop me going to church – to which I probably owe him a great debt and can now bury the Williams with the Good News Bible and the weirdo strangers I used to sit and pretend to read it with on Sunday mornings.

If those come across as deliberately sad examples of man's early love for the motor car, they aren't meant to be. But the old adage that you don't know how much you love something until it is taken away from you is absolutely true, especially when our brains and personalities are still developing. How do we know what really matters to us? How do we know we're not choosing to please our parents, or our siblings, or to cement a friendship we suspect wouldn't be offered unless we feel like we're presenting a common passion, when we know full well we're acting? I liked toy cars, in fact I liked anything cars as a kid – but very few of my friends did. They liked bikes and cricket and hockey and many of the other things I enjoyed. But not cars.

Scalextric was the death of the honest toy car for any boy of my age. Lazy folk choose the metaphor of turning left on an aircraft to describe never going back to a lesser lifestyle, but the Scalextric analogy is the one matters here. I had a magical box of four-wheeled friends and I spent all of my time out on manoeuvres with them, even at the beach, and then one day this black, electrified track arrived and, boom!, I'd moved on faster than Buzz Lightyear could consign Woody to the box under the bed. First there were Minis – one of which was called the Mad Hatter, which meant absolutely nothing to a child who hadn't heard of *Alice in Wonderland*. Then some stock cars, then the Williams my beloved bastard dog Toby ate, and then came the main event: the police Rover with the headlamps and flashing blue lights.

It's both hard and disappointing to try and recall the joy we found in toys. The difficulty lies in being able to remember the events themselves – that's difficult enough if your brain is like mine, the further stretch being able to recall how that felt. But even though I struggle to remember events in the early 1980s, I know full well that the first time I drove a Ferrari – a 550 Maranello – it made me tingle in all manner of ways, but it didn't compare to waiting for the light to fade, and then watching the Rover SD1 police car's lights peer through the gloom, lap-after-lap. That's the disappointing bit – realising that maybe, despite a life so full of automotive experiences and adventure, I've always known that very few things could ever match the raw sense of happiness I felt as a kid. It was magical, that Rover – getting into a groove, understanding the weight of that finger-throttle and then, as the rhythm built, deliberately pushing a little harder, trying to make the rear tyres slide. I just loved it. I'd keep going until those metal brushes that connected vehicle and track were totally worn away. Curiously, I didn't need anyone to race against – an observation we'll doubtless have to scrutinise in future chapters. A child playing alone, in the dark, with an electrified toy police car. Reads like a cry for help to me, but it really isn't. I wasn't a lonely child at all. I had loads of friends and many of them are still my friends today – but secretly it was always about the cars.

Perhaps what defines the car-saddo condition is not being able to recall a time when the toy-car era of your life actually ended. Because for us sufferers, it never does.

The radio-controlled car did to the Scalextric what the Scalextric had done to the toy car. Now these really were life-changing for me. They were the greatest toys of the 1980s – in fact they were the greatest toys of all time – fast machines that you had to build yourself and which were controlled by radio signals and therefore completely wireless. Before I delve into just how wonderful these were, I need to indulge in some feeble catharsis. It's 1984, and I'm desperate for the man previously known as Father Christmas to give me a radio-controlled car for Christmas. What he actually gives me is a remote-controlled car – something with a small motor and batteries, but whose controller is connected by a cable. The operator follows a remote-controlled car where it goes.

My best friend James also wanted a radio-controlled car for Christmas. James lived next door. He was also equally spoilt and lived an equally privileged existence. When we met on Boxing Day to reveal the extent of our spoiltness (we're almost at Little Lord Fauntleroy suits here, we were that fortunate), James produced a radio-controlled car called the Holiday Buggy made by a company called Tamiya. It was the absolute dog's bollocks – more impactful than him rocking up in a Bugatti Chiron now. I was as pleased as any nine-year-old would be at his best pal having comprehensively out-gifted him, and probably didn't hide my envy. He was about as impressed by my slightly rubbish remote-controlled car as I was, and I remember him asking what car it was modelled on. 'A Matra Rancho,' I told him. I used to walk around following a small French MPV whose quirky design would one day lead to the Renault Espace. That's the consolation of being some-one who has a good grasp of French spaceframe technology in the mid 1980s – you can twist any anecdote into demonstrat-ing your impressive and completely useless car knowledge, even when the story is attempting to conceal how spoilt and ungrateful you were. Sorry, Dad.

And true to form, my incredibly generous parents gave me a Tamiya car the following year. It was an Audi Quattro. You'll think this is ridiculous, but that toy car did change my life. You bought the car as a kit and assembled it yourself. For a nine-year-old it was incredibly complicated, and I suppose the intention was that younger kids would build them with their dads (mums didn't do that back then). But my father just wasn't interested, so my much older brother tried to build it with me. Between us we did a poor job, and that Audi never did run that well. But I learnt pretty quickly, and because the cars were genuine scale models I started to connect words I'd read with actual components. This is the point at which I should bemoan the fact that I wish my father had been into cars and we'd hung out in his beautifully organised shed, and he'd taught me how to build a racing car with his bare hands. But that wasn't the case. He was a white man who adopted a small brown kid in 1975. That was a brave thing to do in his social circle back then. That he wanted to play cricket and found my obsession with cars utterly uninteresting is perfectly understandable. And besides, if you build a Tamiya car on your own, you get to drive it 100 per cent of the time.

More Tamiya cars arrived – a Hornet, a Boomerang and a couple of others – over the next few years. I modified them and made then go very fast, and I remember those times as being happy and simple. So many hours went into prepping those wonderful machines compared to how long they actually ran for. They used quite powerful motors and basic nickel-cadmium batteries, so you were lucky if you'd get 15 minutes from a charge. I had two batteries, and they took several hours to recharge, so a full morning fixing things would result in 30 minutes of running, during which time you'd almost certainly hit something and have to un-bend it. This was the complete opposite of instant gratification, and it means that everyone who rightly observes that I'm the most impatient man ever born has no idea that if Tamiya hadn't entered my life I would probably now be under some kind of medical supervision.

Fast forward many years and I have just accepted a job on something called *Top Gear*. I am also racing a Bentley in the biggest sports car championship in the world. The only problem is that due to the unique way the BBC is funded I am not allowed to accept any money as sponsorship for the team. But I still want to have a few names and logos on my crash helmet so I don't look friendless and sad, so I have to think who I'd happily give valuable space to, for free. It took about five seconds to think of Tamiya – so I phoned their UK arm and asked if I could, to which they said, 'how nice'. They even send me the occasional kit, which they still make, and I build them with my kids. I'll have that name on my crash helmet for as long as they allow because it reminds me of how much I learnt making those cars.

TWO
WHAT CAR?
APRIL 1982

Small Street deserves the name. It is less than 300 metres long and I suspect most Bristolians don't know it even exists. There's a couple of bars and there used to be a tiny newsagent, but the majority of it buttresses the legal courts and office space. Without Small Street I probably wouldn't be sitting here about to write this. If anyone was bored enough to untangle the plot of my life and define that one moment – like a middling Thomas Hardy novel – when the course was changed, they would alight on a Saturday morning some time in the spring of 1982.

My late father had his office on Small Street. As a six-year-old I couldn't stand the place. My brief exposure to other-dad workplaces revealed swanky modern architecture and space, but this was the complete opposite – a grim little cupboard that backed on to a tangle of barristers' chambers. I can still smell the damp walls and the cheap upholstery. I still have the creaky hole punch that sat on his desk. I didn't like the place. I now know that this building was the oldest commercial space in the southwest of England. It was riddled with charm and history, and now I'd kill to have my desk in there. But, as I said, to a six year-old it was not cool, and smelt suspiciously like the school toilets.

Saturday wasn't a workday for my father, so we must have been running errands, or most likely have just completed one of his cash-and-carry runs. He was an accountant with a reasonable-sized firm, and the office had a kitchen which he kept stocked with biscuits. Others might have seen this as altruistic, but the truth is it granted him a cash-and-carry card, which were strictly trade-only back then, so he could keep catering quantities of his favourite Club biscuits at home. He was an old dad, well into his 50s, and I was adopted and mixed-race, so we kind of stood-out in early-1980s Bristol because he was well over six foot and white. How he ever thought the people that worked at said cash-and-carry didn't smell a rat when he parked his brand-new white BMW 323i next to all the Transit vans, then wandered in with his little brown kid, I will never know. He would go in, load up a trolley with Club biscuits (always Fruit, Orange and Mint), then transact with his extremely well-spoken voice. We must have looked like a *Fast Show* comedy sketch. I just hope they had plotted the frequency of our visits, could accurately identify the next one, and had some joy in watching us: 'Lads, the tall one that sounds like royalty and his brown kid are back on a biscuit run!'

Boot full of coffee-time confection, we went to Small Street. I assume I was offered the chance to hang out in the smelly office, but didn't want to. I remember he was parked on a double-yellow and asked me to nip in if a traffic warden arrived, and my payment for this sentry work was a magazine he'd just bought from the little newsagent opposite his office. It was a copy of *What Car?*, and once he'd gone off on his biscuit run I remember scanning through the first few pages and thinking this is actually pretty dull because I'm just not that interested in the fact Ford will soon launch a car that looks like a bar of soap and is called a Sierra.

As a six-year-old I wasn't consciously aware in what form I liked cars, but I certainly knew then that I found them fascinating to a degree that was beyond anyone else I had contact with. The frame of that passion was probably quite limited – I would watch the Grand Prix on television, I had many toy cars and a Scalextric track, and I also had a deck of Top Trumps. The importance of the latter on the direction my life took was probably lost on me until quite recently. I've always known how much I loved playing Top Trumps, but it was the nerd aspect of absorbing the numbers that defined motor cars that first drew me in. And that's why my initial exposure to *What Car?* wasn't the epiphany I might have wanted it to be. I do remember sitting there, leafing through the news section, not understanding much of it, not being much interested in the rest of the 'tests', and then coming across the data section at the back. That's when things changed.

The back of *What Car?* contained a list of every new car on sale in the UK at the time. It was an exhaustively complete resource for the price and specification of not only each car but individual models, and there was also some basic performance data available – a top speed and a 0–60mph time. I only recall little bits about that day, but I vividly remember it dawning on me that I now had at my disposal a tool that could settle some of the conundrums that existed in my head that I had never shared with anyone else because I correctly feared that they'd think I was mad. Like many formative car geeks, I would sit in my parents' car at the traffic lights and see, say, a Golf GTI next to a Mitsubishi Colt Turbo and assume that the Golf would smoke the weird-looking Japanese thing because, well, it was a Golf GTI. But now I had a book, an actual oracle of automotive facts that told me the exact opposite was true – the Golf would get smoked.

We drove home in silence, as we normally did, but instead of me looking out of the window and anticipating all the points at which Radio 3 long wave would be interrupted by a bridge or a power line, I buried my head in the back pages of that magazine, blissfully unaware that it was possibly the most important moment in my life. And that's not just because it confirmed that I already had an unnaturally close relation-ship to the motor car, but that my brain didn't quite work the way it was supposed to.

At this stage, academically I was considered to be 'reasonably bright'. This was mainly because I'd learnt that most basic of tricks – sit in front of the teacher, nod a bit, smile, and generally make them like you – and unless you're a complete idiot, you'll probably get by. There was an obvious danger to this strategy when deployed by me – I didn't understand half of what the teachers were saying, I pretended to read books when I couldn't, and as for mathematics, crikey. Put it this way: I didn't see numbers, I just saw odd shapes on a page. Absorbing the data pages of *What Car?* was the first time numbers had made sense to my child brain. I began to see patterns, and I was actually interested in what they represented. My academic mathematics career was shoddy. Fast forward ten years and I'd be having hours and hours of extra tuition to get me through maths GCSE with the lowest grade allowable. And yet if you'd interrupted that exam – one that I still didn't really understand despite all the hours of cramming – and asked me to recite the 0–60mph, 0–100mph and top speeds of the BMW 5 Series range, I would have asked, 'Do you just want manual transmission times, or the autos too?'

But school was different back then, so no one even thought to make a connection between a brain that might operate a little differently if stimulated by something that actually interested it. It goes without saying that this six-year-old wasn't thinking that way when he returned from the Club-biscuit run to his bedroom and spent the rest of the afternoon reading the data pages of that magazine. I do wonder if either of my parents actually spotted what was going on – I'd never read anything that wasn't compulsory for school work, so the fact that I suddenly immersed myself in some written content must have presented as a bit strange. They're both long gone now and I never discussed it with them, but the fact that I was gradually allowed to buy a few more car magazines over the following six months must mean they did spot something.

After that came car brochures. Not because they were any more interesting, but they were more appealing because they were much easier to understand and the pictures were all in colour. There was a small cupboard in my bedroom where these were kept, and I read them every day. Looking back it sounds bizarre, but that's what we did as kids – honed in on the stuff we liked and didn't give a fig about being bored through repetition. This was a time when I had one music cassette and Father had just bought something called a 'video recorder'. Again, I was allowed one tape, and that contained *Live and Let Die*. Accordingly, by the summer of 1982 I could tell you all of the allowable trim combinations for the E24 BMW 6 Series, I knew more about Vauxhall's Cavalier range than the majority of its sales force and thought Jane Seymour was quite the most beautiful woman on the planet. I still have that copy of *What Car?* somewhere.

THREE
SCHOOL RUN

I won't lie, I always went to posh schools. I didn't know they were posh until later in life, but there were a few early signs that things weren't entirely normal – one of them being the lift-sharing situation between mine and two other families.

Some background. My father didn't ever confess to liking cars, but he clearly liked having a nice one. Is that the definition of being middle class? Every two years a new BMW 323i would appear, the old one being chopped-in as a part exchange at the Bristol BMW dealer called Western Counties. I still have the invoices for these purchases, and they reveal that this was as much a financial decision as a need to be seen in something flash. BMWs were rare and expensive in the early eighties, but they also didn't depreciate much – being an accountant he'd clearly prepared some depreciation curve and identified that if he did 24,000 miles over two years he would strike the optimum value outcome. So I went to school in a

323i, which would have been unusual at the local school, but at the posh school it was probably middling at best.

One of the other families had a BMW too. It was a 518 – not even the injected model – and I always remember the fuel flap being under the boot lid, and I know that, like me, you assume it must have been the E12 model. So we had one slightly flash BMW and one slightly blue-collar BMW for three five-year-olds to go to school in. But the other family were in a slightly different league, and their cars blew my mind. There were very special BMWs and Porsches and other treats. I would lie awake at night knowing that it was the turn of the family with the flash cars to drive us the following day. For someone with my condition, that was so exciting I couldn't even think straight. Families with a fleet of very expensive cars are now commonplace, but they weren't back then.

Mostly we'd go in wonderful big BMWs, 735is with in-car telephones and leather that smelt like you were sitting inside an expensive handbag. I'd hear these cars from inside my parents' house and dash out to see which one had arrived. Then one day I heard a very different noise. It was lower in the register and the burble seemed more urgent than anything I'd heard before. I scurried outside and there was a brand new Porsche 928S. This was 1981, so it wasn't the very early egg-shaped car – this had the little rubber rear spoiler and the wider wheels. It remains for me the best looking of all the 928s – that scary grin is perfection – and it looked like nothing else on the road. It also cost well over £25,000 at a time when that sum would have bought a decent-sized house.

The 928 is a little four-seater with very little leg room. In geek motoring circles it's categorised as a '2+2'. This is supposed to denote that the rear two seats are, at best, for children under the age of eight. I'd love to meet the individual who decided that calling something a '2+2' denoted a quite different set of seating proportions to a '4' and shake his hand for selling the motoring community the greatest load of nonsense that could be summoned from a few numbers. Anyway, my friend was in the front seat and he jumped out to fold the seat forwards and let me into the back. The rear seats of a Porsche 928 are unquestionably the coolest ever produced. Please google this immediately to confirm as much.

Snuggled into the back seat of this spaceship Porsche, we headed down into the village to collect our other friend. Now, Chew Stoke is a nondescript North Somerset village. It comfortably loses the popularity contest with its arch-rival and neighbour Chew Magna because it is nothing like as pretty. And, even though it scores highly in the 'silly name' category, it can't begin to compete with the neighbouring Nempnett Thrubwell. What Chew Stoke does have in the list of things that make Somerset villages some of the most baffling and amusing places to live is a ford. English readers will know this is a place where a river crosses a minor road at high water. American readers will wonder why they named it after a car. Most of the time the stream burbles under the road, but when it rains, and it really rains in Somerset, this is the angriest ford I've seen – a 'right bastard' as one of the pub locals once called it. You might have an idea where this is heading in the context of a very low-riding sports car.

Sure enough, it had been raining the night before and was still tipping it down, as per the other 320 days of the Somerset year. We approached the ford from the south side and my friend's dad eyed up the proposition. We had travelled half a mile from my house and were 200 yards from our destination. There were two other routes immediately available that would have removed the water hazard completely from our list of journey obstacles. But I think this dad chose to do what many dads do – he succumbed to the dual temptation of infant lobbying (Go on! Drive through it! Pleeeeeeeese!) and the goading of his own inner-child. For whatever reason, this very successful man chose, as he sat a few inches off the ground in a brand-new Porsche, to accept the challenge of the right-bastard ford.

I now know a little bit about wading a car through water, having done it on most continents, and can safely say that in this case the driver was lacking some technique. Instead of nosing in gently and building a clean bow wave he attacked the swirling mass of chocolate water with surprising aggression, and almost immediately I can remember that mighty V8 roaring harder than it had for the previous half-mile and then feeling that the car was moving a little to the side. We were floating. What I don't remember next is whether any water came into the car, because we were too busy wondering why that musical 4.7-litre V8 was now silent, the noise being replaced by the forlorn moan of a weakening starter motor as my friend's dad attempted the impossible: restarting an engine that has ingested many pints of muddy Somerset water.

The car stopped shimmying with the water flow as its tyres touched the road and we just sat there. I don't think either of us two children said anything because it was hard to tell if the steam surrounding the car was actually coming from his father's ears. One thing I will say is that this adult didn't use a single naughty word as it dawned on him that he'd probably made an unwise choice – if it had been me at the same age the occupants would have learnt some colourful new words.

At this point I can offer advice to anyone who might need it on how to extricate themselves and two six-year-old kids from a Porsche V8 2+2: remove shoes and socks, then wade to the other side. When at the other side, turn and look at the semi-sunken Porsche 928 and think, 'That's a lovely looking machine.' And whatever you do, don't make reference to the white Lotus Esprit in *The Spy Who Loved Me* as the car that might have been more suitable for this particular adventure. I didn't say that, obviously, but I remember thinking it.

So we arrived at our friend's house on foot, carrying our shoes and socks. Which must have confused the mum somewhat, but not as much as there being no car to complete the actual task at hand – driving us to school. I have to assume what happened next is that a call was made by the owner of the semi-aquatic Porsche, because about ten minutes later a mint BMW 735i arrived being driven by the family chauffeur.

CHAPTER THREE

We all jumped in and – from memory – I don't think we were even late for school. If anyone ever tells you that money doesn't make life easier, they're lying.

FOUR
CAR TELLY

Was *Top Gear* the centre of my television universe as a kid? It was certainly a large part of it – Chris Goffey and William Woollard resting one leg on the bumper of something sporty and revealing, as they told us what was 'coming up next week', a little too much of what those Farah trousers were packing. Of course, I loved *Top Gear*, and I used to scurry to the telly the moment I heard the theme tune. But I suppose being young and simple, the sight of an orange Dodge Charger captured my imagination more, as did a bunch of odd people who were on the run from the law, driving around and hiding in the most recognisable van ever built.

The Dukes of Hazzard was Saturday evening for me. Plate of food from Mum, glass of Panda Cola, skids, jumps and the first woman most of my generation fell in love with: Daisy Duke. Of course, it all looks quite ridiculous now, but 'dem Duke boys' set me on my path to being known as the bloke who couldn't drive a car without wanting to slide it around.

I also loved the Grand Prix on BBC Two, but there was something about Hazzard County that I found captivating as a nine-year-old but couldn't have understood. It wasn't the humour, or the legs, or the denim shorts, or the fact that we were supposed to believe that Enos was an acceptable name. Or even what is unquestionably the finest theme tune of its generation. It was the way the cars were driven. Bo and Luke couldn't pop into town for a pint of milk unless they were absolutely sideways – the General Lee must have had the strongest locking differential known to mankind because it was constantly on the lock stops. I just loved it. Surely no other TV show has ever contained more sideways action than that? The Charger was on opposite lock most of the time, and whatever Rosco and co. drove was doing the same. Thank God there were still enough dirt roads in the 1980s to film this stuff. On asphalt they wouldn't have stood a chance to reach those angles unless Hazzard was rainier than the Amazon basin.

So, without realising, I was magnetically drawn to stuff sliding around – to seeing people applying counter-steering. I was uncouth, a fledgling yobbo who was seduced by slip angles and would go on to wreck tyres and annoy many people who think sliding cars is just plain immature. Thankfully I had no idea what a Confederate flag was.

And the driving was, for the most part, real. Occasionally they'd speed something up or cheat the landing after a jump. But the beauty of the General Lee is that it was just a car, so moronic nine-year-olds like yours truly didn't expect it to do anything more than get the boys out of trouble with the law, force Daisy to reveal plenty of thigh and win the occasional race.

But if a car had superpowers, that would present the action-driving department of any television network with some issues back in 1982. I can vaguely remember seeing the trailer for a new TV series on ITV for something called the Knight Industries Two Thousand. A car that could jump and talk and in the most part save the world. *Knight Rider* should have been my favourite television show of all time. For the kid who spent a good deal of his time playing on his own with toy cars and imagining scenarios in which they went on missions and generally over-reached their limited abilities, I must have thought that *Knight Rider* was made specifically for me and produced somewhere in my mind. Many others probably felt the same.

Michael Knight appeared and of course I loved it. But it was so ridiculous from the start that even a seven-year-old struggled to deploy enough immaturity to believe what was going on. There were probably times during my stunning career at Oxford Brookes when I'd have liked to be asked by the suitably progressive English department to deconstruct *Knight Rider* in the context of my emerging pre-pubescent cognisance. The results would doubtless have made fascinating reading for not one human being. And what I would have wanted to say, without knowing it, was that there weren't any decent skids in *Knight Rider*. Not that my field chair at Brookes would have known what a skid meant beyond a gusset-damaging incident.

I'll accept that there was a turbo button and KITT sounded like a Californian doing an impression of Kenneth Williams, and it could jump and was made from something harder than Arnie. But none of that mattered to this nine-year-old, because what I wanted to see was sliding. And as much Patricia McPherson as possible. I still have my 1983 *Knight Rider* annual, but thought better of keeping too much *Dukes of Hazzard* memorabilia around the place. We did have a goose a few years back that I called Uncle Jessie because I felt their waddling walks were similar, but sadly he became Christmas lunch.

A kid is willing to suspend reality up to a point, and of course I watched every single episode of *Knight Rider*, and when Stringfellow Hawk started out-climbing F-16s in *Airwolf* I was there, chomping on beans-on-toast and loving every minute. The people who wrote the theme tunes for all of that 1980s American nonsense were utter geniuses. Even the most laughable of the lot, *Street Hawk*, had a decent catchy tune, but not enough to overcome the absurdity of us being told that an all-terrain motorcycle could do 'over 300 miles per hour'. I was stupid and gullible, but there are limits.

Looking back, though, the fascination with the rear axle of a car travelling further than the front was pretty consistent. The BBC was still showing selected rounds of the British Rallycross Championship in the eighties and that was pure gold for me. It was the format from the gods – cars that looked like normal cars but with silly amounts of horsepower, sideways absolutely everywhere, with those high-level brake lights glowing and all sorts of drama. It always baffles me that rallycross didn't become a huge sport – it has everything.

But the eighties version was so cool – 700hp BMW E30 M3s battling a load of ex-Group B rally cars with Will Gollop and Martin Schanche duelling it fully sideways. Again, the appeal for me was seeing drivers working with absurd slip angles. Unfortunately, the Formula One I knew didn't have any real sliding, and when it did it was barely perceptible on screen. Ground effect was the prevailing technology by then and you rarely saw drivers hanging the arse out of stuff because it wasn't quick and no one had the minerals to showboat in a 1200hp reaper with the throttle progression of a clicked finger.

BBC rallycross coverage was just brilliant, though – there's a load of it on YouTube and I insist that you stop reading this crap immediately and go and watch some. Murray Walker wrestling with fiendishly difficult Scandinavian names and a feast of celebs from outside the muddy world of rallycross – ex-F1 racers like Jonathan Palmer and even television's own Tiff Needell. These boys were fully committed, and however much I loved Formula One (initially Piquet and Brabham, but very quickly Nigel Mansell) there was something so much more exciting about the language of those rallycross cars than single seaters. They slewed about all over the track, their front suspension compressing horribly under braking and then squatting back comically as they surged towards the following corner. I had to go to school on Saturdays from the age of nine and therefore couldn't watch rallycross on *Grandstand* anymore. Mostly I loved school, but when my mum asked me what I missed about being at home I said, 'On Saturdays I miss the rallycross.' Nothing like making your mother feel completely unloved.

If theme tunes remain the ultimate trigger for those memories, there's one that stands above all the others for me – 'Jewelled' by Propaganda. Apologies to non-UK readers because this next bit might not make much sense. The BBC would make a show around what was called the RAC Rally every year, and that music signified it was time to watch my heroes duke it out in UK forests. It was the highlight of my life back then. The *Top Gear* presenting team would lurk about in Rally HQ and there would be a fantastic preview rammed with sideways action and flat-vowelled Finns sounding deeply unimpressed with their abilities to slide among the trees at over 100mph. I think before I was ten I didn't know there was a full championship of events; I just assumed the RAC Rally was a one-off.

Rallying is almost invisible these days, but the crowds back then were enormous. Millions of people watched in the forests. Obviously it was impossible to cover the whole event as it was over a thousand miles, as far south as Bath and all the way up in the Scottish forests, but the BBC did a fantastic job of keeping us enthralled. Do you remember those stately home stages at the beginning of the event? The Beeb would load them up with cameras and we'd see all manner of silliness as the big names drove with remarkable aggression in some very rich person's garden. There was more action in Tony Pond's 1984 onboard from the first stage of the RAC than most entire F1 seasons. He bungs a massive and wholly unsuitable Rover Vitesse around something that looks a bit like Downton Abbey and then stuffs it straight into a tree. It was magnificent to watch back then, and still is now. And that's before we even discuss Tony Mason.

Tony was actually an RAC winning co-driver in 1972 with Roger Clark, and to my generation he was also a kind of northern Murray Walker, but his career mistake was working in a form of motorsport where the cars had two seats and he'd have to ride shotgun. Murray couldn't sit next to Nigel Mansell in a Williams FW14B for obvious reasons. Actually, that must be one of the car community's greatest losses – just imagine Murray absolutely on-the-limiter as Nigel bungs it into the Parabolica at 140mph, shrieking '****ing stop it Nigel or there's a good change I'll s**t myself!!' Anyhow, the hapless Mason would be given several chances to become re-acquainted with his previous meal, as a rally legend hooned through a test stage. I just adored BBC *Rally Report*. I still play the tune by Propaganda most weeks.

That was my rallying fix for the year. Amazing to think that was all we were allowed. There was a preview, a nightly update and then a final broadcast for the results and that was it. I didn't want it to end. And I should probably now admit that part of the reason I felt aggrieved was the amount of television time dedicated to other sport. There was so much football on, but I couldn't stand football. Why did they get something every weekend, whereas I had the F1 races (the calendar was much, much shorter back them and some races were not covered) and the RAC Rally. And a dash of rallycross.

Being denied what you want to watch often just forces you to look harder for similar content. That's why YouTube is such a fantastic resource for car lovers: there are hundreds of hours of all the stuff I was desperate to see as a kid but simply couldn't find. With no internet, you had to box clever. You had to watch films because they contained digestible car content. In a world where all I did was read about cars in magazines and memorise performance data, there was so little available footage of cars moving. Automotive marketing must have been such a confusing industry to work in back then because companies were selling something designed to excite people by the way it moved using mostly static materials. We'd get the odd telly advert, but mostly it was brochures and magazines.

And films. Ever since I'd heckled my mother to rent *Condorman* because I'd seen what looked like a fake Porsche 935 in a trailer (it was utter tripe), I realised I might be looking for different things in films than my friends. *Weird Science* is an especially egregious eighties film based mainly around the pneumatic qualities of Kelly LeBrock's chest, but to 12-year-old me it contained actual, moving footage of a Porsche 928S (not in a Somerset Ford) and a Ferrari Mondial. I'd be lying if I said I didn't notice the leading lady's curves, but if I had to list the respective chassis in order of performance, they would run: Porsche, Ferrari, LeBrock. This is the stuff that matters.

It's why I love *Octopussy* despite it being one of the worst Bond films ever made. It has a driving sequence with an Alfa GTV that's so well-shot and executed with such fine driving that the rest of the film doesn't really matter. Actually, the E28 BMW police cars are excellent too.

The Lamborghini Jalpa in *Rocky IV* is as important as Apollo Creed dying. The BMW M5 and the Audi S8 are the stars of *Ronin*, not De Niro – all of these things are true to the absolute car tragic. I know that now, but I didn't back then. I was a young chap with an insatiable appetite for anything cars, desperately looking for car content to feed the appetite. And that inevitably meant viewing the outside world through the prism of cars, which will sound plain odd to most people, but will hopefully have a few of you nodding and smiling.

FIVE
MUM

Middle England had a standard template of car ownership between parents when I was young. If you were lucky enough to be a two-car family, the dad probably owned and drove the nicer of the two cars – it was faster, more luxurious and normally more expensive. Your mother was more likely to be lumbered with something ordinary and boring in anticipation of it being covered in infant vomit and dog hair and the general fallout from transporting kids. This was exactly the case for my family. I didn't realise it at the time, but the car distribution model was probably the only 'ordinary' thing about the Harris family as I grew up.

Anyhow, as I've already mentioned, my father was an older, professional type who liked to drive small BMWs. Not because he had any real interest in the way they drove, but partly through perceived status and partly because they were simply better built and more reliable than other cars.

CHAPTER FIVE

It's easy to forget, now that most cars are so reliable, people paid a premium for BMW and Mercedes not just because they wanted to look flash, but because they had a better chance of completing journeys.

The other given was that your dad drove fast, and your mum probably didn't. These are now such outdated stereo-types it seems ridiculous typing them, but this odd hierarchy of perceived speed – or maybe even more awkwardly, allow-able speed – was the way the world worked. Kids around the country would be persuaded by Dad not to tell Mum how fast he was driving.

For me it was completely the other way around. My mother was the fast driver. Yes, she almost always had the crappier of the two cars, but on any road other than a dead straight motorway, my father wouldn't have seen where she'd gone, even in his BMW which had twice the power.

The basics of how she became such a good driver are straightforward – she used to race in the late 1950s, and she was pretty good. The details are less clear because she chose not to speak too much about that part of her life. Her racing years were mainly in what was called autocross – these were usually single-venue competitions, and the few cups I found of hers must demonstrate that she was pretty handy.

The highlight of the school week was being collected by my mother – but with her driving my father's car. Then I knew we were in for some fun. School was in Bristol and home was about ten miles south, seven of which were pretty good roads. I'd sit in the passenger seat, goading her to go faster, or to overtake a car, and she'd grin and we'd cover ground at a speed I think very few other mums were achieving at that time. She could pedal those BMWs and the fast Audis my father owned after he retired far better than he could – they danced through corners and did things he didn't even know were possible. I was immensely proud of the fact that my mum could drive so much faster than anyone else's, but this also left me a bit bewildered by all the talk of men being fast drivers. Yes, I knew that all the Formula One drivers were men, but when it came to driving on the road I assumed that all mums were the quick ones because that was how it worked in my family.

Without realising it, this was my first exposure to hilarious sexism and men being pathetically inadequate. My mother would overtake some chap in his fancy car, and as they were being 'done' they'd spot it was a 50-year-old woman and take great offence. Normally they'd give chase, but rarely manage to keep up. I'd be whooping from the passenger seat and loving every minute of it. And when we got home she'd lean over, grin, and say, 'Just don't tell your father.' I can still hear her saying it.

Sometimes this landed us in trouble. I can remember being followed home by some angry, emasculated man who stopped outside our house and remonstrated about her driving. Yes, she was probably way over the speed limit, but for all his huffing and puffing, what he really wanted to say was, 'I'm just upset because I was overtaken by a woman.' I think my teenage children refer to it as being 'butt-hurt'. And what sort of bloke follows a woman back to her house in a situation like that? Quite.

Then there was the time she nearly landed herself in a real pickle. She had collected me from school one Saturday to take me to the county hockey trials. Just typing that sentence I know that if Pad and Fred bother to read this they'll send me messages along the lines of 'posh prick'. But I was from the posh school and I played hockey, and I'm not about to hide that because McGuinness wouldn't have much material to take the piss if I did. I loved hockey nearly as much as cars.

So, Mother collects me from school wearing some fancy frock. I'm 16 at this point, so she's getting on for 60, and her dress code is a West-Country fusion of Barbara Cartland and Joan Collins. She's driving my father's Audi Quattro. She apologises for being a bit late on account of being at a garden party, to which I point out that she's massively late and I want to get into the county team and she'd better pin it. We need to get from Clifton to a place called Winterbourne, where the trials are taking place, in record time. She gives me the don't-tell-your-father grin and then she starts that lovely five-cylinder motor. The route takes us out through the centre of Bristol and on to the M32, the dual carriageway that links good old Bris with the M4. Today it's all confusing 30/40/60 limits, but back then it was national speed limit the moment you drove past St Pauls.

Now, I was pretty accustomed to her getting a move on, so the idea of her accelerating to 90 straight away was perfectly normal – maybe 100 if she was getting a wriggle on. But there was something more purposeful about her that day, and the needle kept rising. It nudged past 110mph as the M32's downhill stretch began – I didn't look at it after that, but the car was still accelerating. The road was empty and I was so comfortable with her driving and loved the feeling of a car built to travel that fast being allowed to do its thing that I just enjoyed the ride. We shot up to the Frenchay turning, darted down the slip road and then headed round the roundabout. That's when I saw the blue lights in the passenger door mirror.

Me: 'Er, Ma, I think we might have a problem.'

Her, really quite excited and jovial: 'Oh yes, dear, that's a police car!'

Now, before we begin with the next bit, you need to hear my mother's voice. It wasn't quite Princess Anne clipped, but it was impressively crisp. So the policeman exits his Cavalier and walks back towards the red Audi, and as the polarising effect of the windscreen dissipates he does a very bad job of hiding the look of astonishment on his face. Thing is, I had hair back then – lots of it, in a kind of wild afro. His eyes definitely darted from me to what he must have assumed was my grandmother. Frankly, he was already undone by the absurdity of the occupants, but I didn't have true confidence to see that at the time and have to assume he was already committed to speaking to us, so had to follow through with the next bit.

Which was to tap on the glass and ask mother to lower her window – the switch to which she couldn't find.

'Blasted thing,' she said as it wound electrically into the door and then with the chirpiness of bumping into an old pal at the golf club continued, 'Hello, officer! can I help you?'

I'll paraphrase the next bit, this coming from 1991.

'Are you aware of how fast you were travelling, madam?'

'No, officer, but this is my husband's car and it does go jolly well.'

'Well, madam, on the downhill section of the M32 my car was showing 110mph, and you were leaving us at quite a rate. I'd estimate you were doing over 130mph.'

'Gosh', she said, sounding more impressed when presented with official confirmation of the Quattro's speed than threatened, as most normal people would be at this point, by a potential custodial sentence.

He then asked her how long she thought the car would take to stop from that speed, to which she did concede 'quite a long way'. And when he politely pushed her for an answer in metres she replied that she only knew yards, then added, helpfully, that she actually used to run the 100 yards quite quickly at school the 1940s. At this point, I thought we might be in proper strife.

But he warned her about the dangers of travelling so fast, actually noted that her driving wasn't in any way erratic, and told her continue with her journey, but with far less speed.

'That was close!' was about the extent of her concern.

Now, there's a bit to digest here. The first is that the 48-year-old me knows she was actually never in trouble because it wasn't a police pursuit car that nabbed us, so it didn't have the ability to clock the exact speed needed for a prosecution. But she didn't have a clue about any of that and just styled it out. If it had been an 18-year-old me driving, the outcome would have been different. Frankly, she was magnificent. I have no doubt that the moment he opened the cop-shop door when he returned back to base, he said, 'You're never going to believe what just happened.'

We did make it to the trials very late, I did score a pretty handy goal, and I did make the team. And, predictably, one kid did note that I was a 'posh prick' as I climbed back into the Audi Quattro with what was clearly a grandma to head home. But who cares when you've just survived a 130mph scrape with the law? Of course, as we rolled onto the driveway: 'Best not tell your father.' And I never did.

Later in life, after my father had died, I made sure she had some fast cars of her own. She loved driving them and she didn't attempt to hide how much she loved the way an old girl in something flash turned heads. There was an Alpina B10 3.3 Touring, then a 535d Touring which, like every other 535d in the land, was mapped to buggery, faster than a stabbed rat and smoked like Dot Cotton.

She was about to sell her Mercedes C32 AMG estate when I was running its replacement, a C55 estate. Now, all you geeks out there will know that there were a few rumours surrounding the new C55. Yes, it had a creamy, normally aspirated V8 instead of the 32's supercharged V6, but some people thought the old car might have been a little faster. And the one rule of the new performance car is that you simply must be faster than your predecessor. We love a bit of scandal in the fast-car world. Anyhow, I can confirm that a 2002 C32 estate will comprehensively dust a 2004 C55 because on the way back from somewhere I came across my then 70-year-old mother at some traffic lights. She was in her C32 and she completely destroyed me in said C55 from a standstill to a speed that, it being 2002 by then and times being a bit more judgemental than 1991, I'd rather not mention.

And she was a great passenger. I have many, many memories of her sitting with me, trusting me, enjoying the speed. Teaching me to drive: to declutch and match the revs. She was shattered when my father died suddenly, and I needed to get her away from home, so we went to France to stay with friends. I asked if she wanted to fly, and she said she'd rather travel in my old, noisy Porsche. I've never told anyone this before, but one of the reasons I love the 1988 Porsche 911 Club Sport so much is that I drove mine through the night from Calais to Nice, with the woman who had adopted me, nurtured me and shown me more love than anyone before or since, sleeping next to me, utterly broken by the loss of her husband. As the sun rose somewhere south of Aix-en-Provence, she woke up and asked how fast we were going. 'About 140,' I said. 'Good,' she said. 'I like this car.'

She rode shotgun in so many of the very fast cars I was allowed to test for magazines and films, and she loved my old Ferrari 512 TR, which she always called beautiful. She never once came to watch me race because she said the klaxon siren that sounds when a car enters the pit lane made her sick to her stomach, and she feared seeing me hurt or killed at a circuit. But I know she was proud of the few pots that I won along the way.

In 2018 she fell off a Segway attempting to show some other old gimmers that she still had it. I mean, how perfect is that? She was so tough, but her body never really recovered from the knock, and other complications emerged. As an act of defiance for both of us in the face of the inevitable, I asked her if it was time to upgrade her lightly tuned Audi S4 Avant for the new RS 4. We specced a silver car together and I went about trying to find insurance for an 84-year-old, which it turns out was nigh-on impossible. She didn't live long enough for the car to be built. Or for me to ask her why she hadn't mentioned the nine points on her licence.

Her last car journey was to the hospital in the back of my Bentley Mulsanne, which she thought was 'ridiculous'. Like many other observations she made about her son and his cars, she was absolutely right. I was with her as she died; I told her the few things I'd done that were worthwhile had only been done in the spirit in which she'd allowed me to go about life. Then I kissed her and said thank you. I miss her every day. No matter how old you are, life is never the same after your mum dies.

SIX
DAD

I'm still unsure if my father was just an average driver, or that my mother was so good that he was made to look less than capable. I suppose I just have to admit that he fell into the standard, rather disappointing category of most male drivers I've met who just aren't as good as they think they are. He also liked to get a decent clip on at times – average skill and above average speed are always a twosome – so journeys could be quite memorable.

My father was an older dad. I think I always knew this but the first time it struck home was during the dad's spring race at junior school as the other dads duked it out and mine was watching, on crutches, after his first hip replacement. He went on to have five more, which I'm told is a record in the UK. My parents adopted me when I was very young, and if my mother, who would be lizarding in the sun given any opportunity, could at the very outside appear to be genetically related to me, the same couldn't ever be said of my father. We looked comically different.

Multi-race families are the norm now, but back in the mid-seventies, in North Somerset, they were not. I can rightly claim to have been 'the only one in the village' and that being compounded by the fact I went to the posh school meant I wasn't about to make many local friends. Unless they also went to posh schools. I've also found out latterly that the village pub was the home of the local National Front, so maybe I should just be thankful I didn't take a massive kicking!

I now realise that I wasn't separated from my father by one generation, but probably by two. He was born in 1932, and when the German bombers could reach Bristol he was sent away to Devon. He must have been seven or eight years old and I'm told he was very close to his mother, and was not emotionally prepared to be separated from her. The first thing the woman who was supposed to look after him did was burn his favourite teddy bear to toughen him up. What an appalling thing to do. Of course he never told me that himself, someone else did. And that probably sums up the way his generation communicated with mine – or didn't, as the case may be.

Nearing 50, I find myself saying, or typing, the phrase 'I learnt too late' about 20 times a day, but I really did in so many cases. One of the thousand things I didn't spot was that my father's generation didn't spill their guts about anything; they appeared to be completely mute and emotionally distant and repressed – the idea of opening up about 'feelings' was so foreign, they'd bristle at the idea of it. But what they did do was share stories about their pasts that at the time seemed utterly dull and meaningless, but which I now understand were deliberately allegorical. They were deployed to give young'uns like me a chance to understand individuals.

Here's one. My grandfather died in 1953, so it stands to reason that I don't know much about him, but it's still quite weird that the only fact I was ever told by my father about *his* father, is that he could float especially well in the sea. Such was his buoyancy, he could read a paper while bobbing about. And that's it – I know nothing more about this man than that one fact, and it does have more than a whiff of bull about it.

So my father wasn't an open book. He was kind and I knew he loved me, and I suppose that's what matters, but he was also someone whose temper I feared and who only spent time with me on his own terms, and that meant two things: playing hockey and cricket. Those two sports were my father's life and he would spend hours giving me chuck-downs to improve my batting or whack a hockey ball about. The only problem was, I preferred cars, and he didn't really like that.

The school run with Father driving was never stress free. There's a hill called Dundry between Chew Stoke and Bristol, and this was his designated overtaking place. He'd wind up the little 323i and then attempt to pass slower traffic. There were two problems with this strategy. The first was his technique – he clearly had a problem with revving the engine beyond a certain rpm, which meant mid-overtake, just as that lovely little six-cylinder motor was about to deliver its best, he'd shift up a gear. It was quite bizarre! And also quite alarming because Dundry Hill is quite steep so the car's acceleration would reduce and we were exposed to oncoming traffic for longer.

The other issue was that this overtaking spot wasn't an especially straight piece of road, nor was it very wide. I drove it a few days ago and found myself wondering why anyone would even attempt to pass a car there! In fact I do that quite a lot now – drive the roads I did when I'd just passed my test and scrutinise the places that I'd decided were 'overtake spots'. Most of them now look like a suicide mission. But they really weren't, and I don't think my dad was a total lunatic either. First off, all cars were way, way smaller back then. Don't underestimate how much more wieldy and placable those old machines were – roads that now feel restrictive and narrow didn't back then.

And cars were so much slower in the eighties – that 323i was one of the faster cars on the road at the time, but it would struggle to stay with a normal hatchback now. You can also assume that the traffic approaching you was also travelling more slowly, so the actual time you had to complete the overtake was much, much longer than today.

I now realise that I have never met a more stubborn man than my father. To what extent that was a function of him being evacuated I will never know, but he expected life to bend towards him, rather than the other way. In fact, he just couldn't see another way. That's not me being harsh, and I think it was true of many men of his generation, to the extent that I don't think he'd even recognise men of today.

With that stubbornness came a need for routine. He lived his life in a kind of *Groundhog Day* repeat that most of us found quaint, and he was willing for those around him to poke fun at this. That's a crucial observation because he did have a great sense of humour and allowed those close to him to observe his quirks and make light of them. You just had to time it right, or else.

I always remember the tomatoes. He had to have a tomato sandwich every evening at about 6.30pm. Followed by a cake. Not sweets, but a cake. Breakfast was always cornflakes and clotted cream with sugar on top – and a new cornflake packet had to be opened a certain way. I was once staying with a friend whose dad handed me a new box of cereal; I asked, 'How do you prefer it to be opened?' and he gave me a strange look.

This obviously transferred to his motor car. When I drive with my kids they are allowed to do pretty much anything short of grabbing the steering wheel or switching off the traction control – although that has happened before, by accident, and created one of the most severe code-browns of my life. They fiddle with everything and choose the music and cock about with the seats and generally do as they please. And I love it. Rewind 40 years, if I so much as touched the heater controls of those BMWs there would be a serious problem. You just didn't mess with your dad's stuff, but now you absolutely do mess with your dad's stuff. What does this mean about society? I have no idea beyond noting that modern cars have far more buttons to play with.

CHAPTER SIX

Back to the quirks. Morning coffee was always served in the same cup and saucer, with one of those Club biscuits. In fact, I have a decent Club-biscuit story, which is not a phrase you hear every day. In the early nineties, McVitie's changed the shape of the Club biscuit (I wouldn't want to be quoted on this, but I think they were made longer and thinner) and it would no longer balance on his favourite cup and saucer. Any normal person at this point would find an alternative method of transporting the biscuit, but not my father. No, he chose to take up his complaint with the customer services department of McVitie's and then escalate it further to some poor manager. Naturally, all of this was written correspondence, and he was happy to share with people that he was locked in a battle with a confectioner over its decision to change the shape of a biscuit. The letters are rather charming and reflect a way of life that seems much further back in time than 30 years ago.

After he'd passed away I had to go through all of his affairs, as any son does. In them I found a few files that recorded other little spats he'd had with products that had been part of his routine, and whose discontinuation had now disrupted the equilibrium of his life. The best of these was an especially lively back-and-forth with Campbell's over its decision to discontinue a particular variety of tinned soup. A similar gripe would now be subject to a Twitter outburst, our method to embarrass the company in question. But back in 1990 it took the form of several very well-written and good-natured letters, the last of which, from Campbell's, told my father to please fuck off and stop wasting their time in the kindest and most lovely manner imaginable.

I was not an easy teenager, so I went off to boarding school largely because my father just couldn't handle me being so difficult. And you know what? He was absolutely right to do that. I was a pain in the arse, and I also wanted to spend all my time at school with my pals, so it suited both parties. This means there aren't many car-related stories because we weren't together in cars very often. It also meant I wasn't present when my parents were on the Isle of Skye and my father filled my mother's petrol-powered Renault Espace with diesel and they remained on the island for many more days than originally intended. From the way it was described, it was probably well avoided.

When the day came to take lessons and pass my test, the uncomfortable truth was that not only could my father not understand my emerging obsession with cars, he viewed it as unhealthy and potentially a threat. Looking back, I can sympathise with his concerns – I flunked most of my exams and ended up going to an ex-poly when all of my other friends achieved far more. He must have been thinking it was his responsibility to help me avoid working in the motor industry, which in those days was seen by professional types as being worse than becoming an estate agent. The sad thing is, I just loved cars, and because of his unbending view of the world, it wasn't something we ever shared. I think we once went to the British Motor Show, but we never went to watch any racing or anything like that. Again, I don't blame him – that's just the way it was. He gave me an amazing education and took me on stunning holidays, and, above all, he adopted me and gave me a seat at the table of very comfortable middle-class England when, frankly, I could have ended up anywhere.

In September 1998 I moved to London to start my first job, at *Autocar* magazine, and I can remember going to say good-bye. He was struggling to be positive because he just didn't think any of it stacked-up on paper. I was being paid £12,000 a year and that wasn't enough to live off in London. I was determined to make my own way, but of course he was right. Six months into the job of my dreams I was financially on my arse because I had been too stupid to realise that taking home £600 against rent of £500 wasn't going to work. I phoned him and he offered to help me with some extra cash while I worked hard to reach a salary point where I could stand on my own two feet. He did it kindly and without ever making me feel like I'd failed. He died a few months later, weeks before *Autocar* promoted me and gave me enough money to not need his help.

His passing shattered me, as it did my mother. The two years leading up to his death had been so much smoother than before. We'd stopped arguing, we played golf together; I think we enjoyed each other's company. In short, I'd grown up a bit and wasn't such an idiot.

I was 24 when he died, and it did change me. Despite not having been especially close to him for much of my life, I was resentful at being left alone. I was confused by the reality of the situation – losing one parent is terrible for anyone, but no one ever tells you that the real pain is seeing the disintegration of the one that's left behind. My mother would occasionally say that my father would have been proud of what I've done, but what else was she supposed to say? I really don't know what he'd have thought. I think he'd be quite baffled by how things panned out: no less so than me.

I suddenly had to grow up aged 24. I was an itinerant, privileged child in a young man's body with few formal qualifications and a job that would barely cover the bills. And, for the avoidance of doubt, I didn't suddenly inherit a load of money. My father was way too smart to leave me much at that age. If there is one upside to being in that position, it's that it freed me from parental judgement when it came to taking risks. If I'd been using his sound advice to decide whether to give it all up to make Drivers Republic, or leave all the comfort of freelance life to start making films on something called YouTube, he'd have rightly told me to be sensible, and stay put. He'd have been right. But both of those reckless moves taught me far more than remaining in the comfort zone. That's one of those glib sentences I hoped I'd never be forced to write, but it's also the thing that gives me hope for the next generation. Because in the tangle of pronouns and other utter nonsense they've tied themselves up in, the one thing they have done is liberated themselves from the fear of change. They are so much better at that than us.

My father left his mark on me in several strange ways, some of them predictable, some not. For me, the apple always lands far from the tree – we're more likely to be a reaction to our parents than be carbon copies. My father was an accountant and a very organised, rigorous man. His monthly bank statements always carried his own calculations of what the balances should be, and most months he was right and the bank was wrong. He managed money to the last penny. I have no idea how much is in my account. Even when I had no money at all, I still didn't look.

I don't have any routines – in fact the thought of having a routine imposed on me is one of the few things that could keep me awake at night. It terrifies me. I want to wake up and do whatever needs doing that day. I don't want to eat the same food on repeat and I'm hopefully a little more proficient at driving a motor vehicle than he was. But I walk the same routes he used to, I take a holiday in the place that he loved and where he passed away, every year, and will do so until I die. I try to sit on the same rock he did every day that I'm there.

I wonder what advice he'd have given me over time, and what he'd make of the life I've led; even though it would be comforting to assume he'd have thought it all some fairy tale, I suspect he'd have thought I was a bit of a loose cannon and never too far from a disaster of my own making. And he'd have been absolutely correct.

SEVEN
CAR MAGAZINE

I'm 12 years old now, and there's a nice little pile of car magazines and brochures and stuff I've scavenged to be stashed in the small cupboard in my bedroom. Imagine a mouse's nest of random items and you'll have the picture. The magazines are mostly *What Car?* because that's what my parents think I like. There's the odd copy of *Motor*, but nothing from the fancy end of the spectrum. For the few normal people out there reading this, allow me to explain.

In the 1980s the car area of the newsstand was a busy place, and it knew its customers very well. To the uninitiated (and uninterested) they all looked the same, normally with a bland image on the front cover and a name that only sounded right when said with the most adenoidal of voices: *Autocar, Car and Car Conversions, Fast Lane, Performance Car.* Whereas *What Car?* was much more of a buyer's guide and probably bought as a one-off by people trying to choose a new car in the pre-internet era, the others pandered to slightly different types of hobbyist – from the real spanner-monkey nerds who prefer it when their MG Midgets don't work, to yuppies who want to know whether the latest Porsche Carrera can out-sprint a Ferrari 328.

I think I was in the old, much-missed WH Smith in Clifton Village when I bought my first copy of *Car Magazine*. It was 1987 and the cover was just too much to ignore. 'There will never be another month like this,' it proclaimed with perfect immodesty. The cover was split into thirds and the images were: a Ferrari F40, a crazy Lamborghini, an Aston Zagato and a Ferrari 288 GTO. Opening this magazine and being transfixed by the pictures was unsurprising, but there was a new element at play here: the words. I wasn't much of a reader back then; I'd scan the odd book if teachers insisted, but this was the first time I really wanted to read large chunks of text. Buying that copy of *Car* probably set my already below-average academic career back several years, but without knowing it, it was the foundation of a passion that would eventually become a job.

After that issue of *Car* I started buying it every month. The writers became familiar: Steve Cropley, Gavin Green and some older chap called George Bishop who seemed to only write about the quality of free food and drink at car launches. He perfected the review that doesn't actually mention the thing being reviewed about a decade before it became a standard format in the Sunday papers. This was a magazine that sold the dream of driving to a boy who was still five years away from being able to drive. To most of my friends it looked a bit odd, especially when I went to boarding school, because literally no one else in a house of 70 boys was really interested in cars. And I know this because if they had been, those car magazines would have been stolen. Anything of any interest was always stolen: booze, cigs, clothes, other genres of magazine. But never my car mags.

In so many ways, I still think life was kinder and simpler back then, but the ability of a young person to indulge in a hobby or passion independently of their peers or parents was so much harder before the internet. Yes, my mother liked driving cars fast, but she didn't get me any access to a community of people I could talk to or learn from. To the school, cars were just a distraction to a pupil who was already lazy and underperforming. I'm not one to look back on my education and whinge, because I was enormously privileged, but if the teacher who (quite rightly) confiscated a car magazine I was reading during prep time could recall that now in the context of what I do for a living, they'd surely cringe just a little bit? I think I would in their position. But the counter-argument is perhaps even more compelling: should teachers and parents indulge in every teenager's latest fad and attempt to nurture it just in case it becomes a career? Probably not. But the unavoidable truth, surely, is that if a kid demonstrates a consistent curiosity for one subject, nurturing that is as important as trying to pass a maths exam.

So, *Car Magazine* became a bible for me. I read it cover-to-cover. And then I reread it. It became a new imaginary world, just like those adventures with toy cars. If you'd asked me before writing this if I was a childhood fantasist, I'd have laughed and said 'no', but clearly I was! This was my community, these were the voices I identified with and – this is hard to write without coming across as a bit strange – these were my friends. I receded to a private world of variable valve timing and double-wishbones. And that's why, when people come up to me and want a chat about a car or whatever, I always try and give them some time. Because I know what it's like to consume content – words or podcasts or films – over time and feel so aligned with the people making it that you instinctively feel like they're your pal. And then when you finally meet them in the flesh it doesn't feel at all like a first meeting. The problem being, for the other person, it is!

When I worked with Matt LeBlanc on *Top Gear*, this behaviour was so concentrated people would talk s-l-o-w-l-y to him because they assumed he was Joey, when of course he's as sharp as a tack.

Anyhow, *Car Magazine* was the boss throughout my teenage years and even into my twenties. What appealed was the storytelling and the distinctive voices. I now know all about the history of the magazine: how it was effectively an Australian invasion by Ian Fraser and Steve Cropley and Gavin Green. But there was no Wikipedia in 1987, so when I was attempting to read a column by someone called L.J.K. Setright, not only did I assume he spoke and wrote a different kind of English to me, I had no idea he was some verbose legend who approached the subject of cars like the more

Victorian of my teachers approached the murkier corners of the literary canon.

I suppose early on I pretended to understand what L.J.K. was chattering on about – Honda Preludes being amazing despite the fact no one else seemed to like them. He would also perpetually compare modern fast cars to Bristols from the 1960s. If my father's ENT consultant hadn't driven one, I wouldn't have had a clue what a Bristol was, nor, in another strange Setright connection to my late father, would I have thought much about Avon tyres unless he'd been the company auditor for many years. The meaning of all that? Because I grew to love the theatrical hey-look-at-me of Setright's prose, his views on cars seamlessly became mine. I'd never driven a Honda Prelude, but I told anyone who would listen that they were great.

Setright was the progenitor of the celebrity car writer. He was BC – Before Clarkson. He wasn't on television much, but I'm told he did occasionally appear on Radio 4 where his main skill wasn't as a commentator of all matters car, but as a concert-standard clarinet player. What stood out about this man wasn't just his strange prose, but the reverence with which he was held by everyone else, especially his fellow writers: this was something new. Whenever there was an especially important subject to dissect, or rivalry that required expert officiating, Setright would be unshackled and 'decide'. The idea of someone's status being elevated because a bunch of nerds appointed a chief nerd to approach a consumer review of two cars (which would look very similar to the untrained eye) with a seriousness most people would reserve for the Israel-Palestine situation is, on reflection, mildly absurd.

But this is the crux of the hobby that becomes an obsession. Once a community builds around anything that most people would find borderline laughable – fishing, model railways, you name it – oddball heroes are created and they fit the mould perfectly. Peak Setright for me was probably a shot of him adjudicating over a bunch of hot hatchbacks, with a cover shot of him studying his copy of the Old Testament as he loomed over those cars he was about to judge. It was completely ridiculous! Or maybe it was an earlier cover designed to seduce us readers into the prospect of a Mercedes S-Class vs Jag V12 vs BMW 750i comparison test whose most prominent image was, yes, Setright's face – not any of the three cars! I just loved it all. I'm laughing at it now, but back in 1988 it was deadly serious, and if you'd asked me who the greatest living Englishman was, I'd have said Leonard Setright.

Two years later and the answer would have been different. No, I'm not trying to demonstrate how fickle the affections of the teenage car magazine reader are, it's just that I was now processing the words differently and forming these creepy one-way allegiances in a more sophisticated way. There was another writer on *Car Magazine* whose style could equally be regarded as self-conscious and over-complicated, but I just loved the way he wrote – it was Russell Bulgin. My English education was typically Victorian and rigid, and here was a writer who allowed himself to play with words and paint vivid pictures. And he celebrated just the type of strange observations that I saw in cars. If a good writer is one that makes you nod at something you think you might have seen the same way as them, a great writer draws you into a subject you assumed he or she is the only person who has ever made that single observation other than you.

Bulgin was the master of this. His monthly column was surgically constructed, and every last word landed. Some people thought him pompous, but I knew the moment I saw his name after a standfirst the words would be sublime. The other mark of the very finest writers is that they really can write about anything – Bulgin introducing us to the man who ensured all Toyotas had adequate rear-window drop to allow a large fast-food drinks cup to pass through it was more entertaining than most other motoring journalists writing about the latest Ferrari supercar.

Fast forward many years and I'm on my first week of work experience at *Autocar* and they've just hired Bulgin from *Car Magazine*. In the myopic little world of automotive media in the mid-1990s, this is like Haas nabbing Lewis Hamilton. The editor has asked me to go to the Chelsea Harbour Hotel to collect some rolls of film from Mr Bulgin. It takes me a few deep breaths in the car park to summon the courage to approach him because he's busy running a pound coin between the panel gaps on the new Lexus IS200, which is Japan's first real attempt to tackle that most German of vehicles, the small sports saloon. He was a very, very tall man, and I'm quite the opposite. I can remember calling him Mr Bulgin, which on reflection is absurd. I was Remy from *Ratatouille*, and he was the great critic Anton Ego, towering above me. Only he was of course far kinder than that. He handed me the rolls of film and went about his business of judging the assembly quality of this new machine by way of the Royal Mint. I met him once more, at a Ford launch in Cannes, and then he fell ill. He wouldn't have known who I was, but to be able to stand and hear him talk about cars, to be allowed the chance to put a voice to the thousands of words of his I'd read in my study bedroom at school, was a joy for me. He died in 2005 and will be remembered by many people for a piece he wrote about Ayrton Senna for *Car and Car Conversions*. A collection of his best pieces was collated into a book after his passing; if you can snag a copy it's quite sublime.

Car Magazine in its pomp was probably the best car magazine that ever existed, or ever will exist. It had enormous influence and it told the most memorable stories. That won't matter to many people, but I love the industry I partly had to leave behind to end up on television, and I'll always want to celebrate those who shone brightest within it. *Car* is still published, but like all of those titles that used to jostle for prominence on the newsstand, it isn't the same. The world has moved on, and so has the car industry – we have YouTube and Instagram and influencers and a load of other stuff that the car industry thinks serves it better and reaches new and important audiences. I don't think any of it is as clever or as enjoyable as good old words and still images – and I include all of my own output in that statement.

EIGHT
RENAULT 21 SAVANNA

I'd wager that not many people have done anything that exciting in a Renault 21 Savanna GTX estate, but I did.

I think I was 12 years old at this point, and had taken to driving my mother's car around the driveway. This sounds much grander than it actually was because the drive wasn't very big, and merely allowed me to practise three-point turns. But I'd have the radio blasting some music and pretend that I was actually a driving god. To this car-obsessed kid, being able to understand how the clutch worked, to allow the clutch plates to nibble away at each other as you found the bite point – well, that was manna from heaven.

Now I'm fairly sure my father didn't approve of me doing this – to the point that it was probably something I only did when he was out. In fact, I don't think he had any idea it had become something of a regular pastime. Again, my ma was being a complete legend and letting me have covert fun. My dad was out watching his old cricket club attempt to win the league. That bit would prove critical later in this story.

I was now so confident in my new-found clutch control that I had my pal Rowan with me, riding shotgun. He was a year older, so what the casual observer would have seen is a couple of kids doing three-point turns, with Belinda Carlisle's 'Heaven is a Place on Earth' cranked up to 11. The fact that I've typed that should confirm that everything in this book is the truth, because that's not something I want to admit.

Anyhow, the driveway to my parents' house was very steep and led to the flat bit on which I was demonstrating my skills. My normal line was to let the car roll forwards with a nip of clutch, then push it straight back in, grab reverse and deftly apply a little brake before gently popping the clutch back out to send the car backwards just before its nose fell down the steep part of the drive. Now you probably think you know what's about to happen, but you don't because I haven't yet introduced the most important character in this little story – a leylandii tree.

Now, this wasn't any ordinary leylandii. It was an absolute bastard of a leylandii – a species which is already about as horrid and invasive and greedy as anything on the planet. It was the thick end of 80 feet tall, had sucked the life out of a significant circumference of lawn around it and rippled the tarmac beyond. The only positive purpose it served was for the two dogs to sleep under when it rained. Other than that, it was a bastard.

So, we're in a blue, D-plate Renault Savanna GTX, the one with the bigger 120hp fuel-injected engine, rolling forwards towards the bit where the drive suddenly dips downhill, and for some reason I will never, ever be able to comprehend, I let the car drop downhill just a little bit further than before. At this point Rowan must have been thinking, 'This is interesting.' I was now in unknown territory. Like Jim Clark experimenting with a Colin Chapman wing, or Michael Schumacher having one of his Friday practice-offs, I was pushing the boundaries of my driving skills and flirting with the low wall that flanked the driveway. Or I was being a dick – one of the two.

What happened next will haunt me forever. No shunt I've had since has made me feel as bad.

As the car began to roll away, all sensible actions betrayed me – I think Rowan shouted, 'Hit the brake,' which would have solved everything, but instead, with the car already in reverse, I allowed the clutch to spring backwards, threw some revs at it and panicked. This solved the immediate problem of clipping the front of Renault's blunt-snouted Cavalier rival into the wall, but the reversal of direction was way too successful. So what had been 5mph of forwards momentum was now 10mph of backwards momentum. And then came the awful scrunch of branches and the pop of tempered glass exploding before it shattered into little cubes and jangled against anything it could. I still don't know why I didn't just dip the clutch and brake. I suppose the answer lies somewhere in the phrase, 'I was 12 years old and couldn't drive.'

Predictably I was not a model of calm in the aftermath. Rowan did a fine job of calming me down, but then the self-loathing began.

The mental response to crashing a car is as interesting to me as it is terrifying. Of course it's happened to me several times since that day, but like other scenarios in life – most of them designed to be more pleasurable – you never forget your first time. Certain things about it have stayed with me forever. The sense that you know something is about to happen and you are powerless to avoid it – that sense of helplessness is something that will always haunt me. These days it's not necessarily a fear unless I think the outcome is going to be life-threatening – it's the elapsed time between the moment your brain says, 'This is now out of our control,' and the moment you hit the thing you wish you weren't going to hit.

It doesn't matter if you're 12 and driving your mum's Renault, or you're 27 and driving someone else's Maserati – when your brain informs you that this isn't going to end well it sends bolts of energy down your spine that fizzle out into your limbs, and they propagate fear and indecision. You shift from being the driver to being a passenger. I probably learnt that the hard way, a little younger than most.

In hindsight, the first thing I remember about my mother's appearance on the crime scene was her generation's stoical resistance of resorting to swearing. She just uttered one of those generic poshy-phrases (cripes/lummy/blimey, etc.) and asked if we were okay. Then the clean-up began.

Actually, first she had to drag the car forwards and away from the clutches of the bastard leylandii and then the clean-up could begin. I was pretty useless by then – a mess of tears and fears about how utterly batshit my father was going to go when he heard about this. And this was one of the few times that I was reminded that my parents really did know each other very well. Once she'd surveyed the mayhem – the back of the car was totalled, the rear windscreen was smashed, one of the rear quarters was badly damaged too – she turned to me and said, 'Forget the car, clear up all the glass on the ground. If the dogs cut their paws it'll be awful and your father will hate that more than the car being damaged.'

Fast forward several hours and we're now at some village gathering, and people are eating and drinking and having fun. I'm shitting bricks about the imminent arrival of my father. There are no mobile telephones, so he can't be forewarned, but he turns up looking mildly sunburnt and in good spirits. That's about all I could hope for at the time. My mother had given me a cheap bottle of Italian fizz to give to him but made sure I had to fess up in person.

'Dad, I've crashed Mum's car.'

'How?'

'I reversed it into the big tree.'

'Right. What's that?'

'It's a bottle for you, to say I'm sorry.'

He puts on his reading specs, sees 'Asti Spumante' and gently pushes the bottle away, like a dog that's just farted on his leg.

And then the key part: 'Is there any smashed glass? Because if there is, the dogs could cut their paws.'

His team had won the league and his dogs were okay. The car was very poorly repaired and sold soon after. But what I didn't realise at the time was how much that incident had adversely affected how my father viewed my obsession with cars. What else was he supposed to think? No wonder after that he would try and do anything to keep me away from them.

NINE
LEARNING TO DRIVE

For the car tragic there are really two lives – the one you lived before passing your driving test and the one you enjoyed after you'd passed.

I don't know the exact date when the potential of driving became an imminent possibility, which is kind of odd because cars had been such a dominant part of my life for as long as I could remember. I think this is partly because I'd separated this weird quest for knowledge about cars – a need to absorb every little piece of information – from the actual process of driving them. Maybe it was partly denial? If something matters so much to us that the thought of it not happening is shattering, then best pop it to the back of your mind and park it there.

But one day I did turn 17, and that meant having the chance to drive legally, on the road. My father bought me a car, a red Mini City, and I was the happiest man-child alive. It was old and a bit shit and probably a death trap, but I didn't care. My mother had raced Minis and the manner in which she spoke about the way they handled and them being such giant-killers made me want nothing else. I remember where me and Ma went for a drive that day after tying on the L-plates, and of course I still head over to those roads every now and again. She was hugely patient, but also quite correct in assuming that I'd need some proper lessons to pass a test.

I learnt to drive with an old chap called John Buckle in Bristol. I can't remember the names of people I met this morning, but I can remember John Buckle and his E-Plate Peugeot 205 five-door with a 1.1-litre engine. It was silver and had the facelift dashboard. There was no great BSM-style plinth on the roof, just some L-plates permanently stuck to the front and rear. I really enjoyed my driving lessons with John. He was a calm man who had that knack, like all the best teachers, of wanting to make you show your very best all the time. And he clearly saw it as his duty to not only get people to pass a test, but make them half-decent drivers.

He used to reserve special praise for finessing each input to the point of seamlessness – especially when braking. 'The goal has to be the passenger being unaware that you've actually stopped.' I still try and do that now. I doubt John is still alive, but if he is I'd like him to know that I still use his 'extra' indication method on the Christchurch roundabout in Clifton. Be a little bit John every day.

So, I have a little Mini and a driving instructor who I think is good at his job – it's all looking good. Better still, my mother has gone in to bat with my father to persuade him that I can lightly modify the Mini. Now this is the early nineties and car insurance for young people is more expensive than flying on Concorde, so I had to be pretty careful what I did – and none of it was meant to allow the car to go faster. So while the good ship Buckle was teaching me how to pass my test, and my ma was taking me out for the occasional trip in the Mini, I ripped out the interior, fitted a set of Cibie lights that would melt the rear of the car in front and fitted a Janspeed exhaust with a centre outlet. I cannot tell you how proud I was of that snake of pipework. I used to go out and look at it before it was fitted. Exhausts are the artwork of the car world. Forget fancy installation pieces, just get yourself an Akrapovič and spend days staring at it.

It goes without saying that this fairy tale was also a bit of a fallacy. My group of friends at school were now well-established, close-knit and absolutely brutal to each other. I wouldn't have had it any other way, but in the context of driving it left a couple of issues to keep me on my toes. The first was being followed on your driving lesson. Having a January birthday meant there were several mates who had already passed their tests and were already independently mobile. Factor in a total disregard for attending lessons and some decent sleuthing, and they would work out where and when your driving lesson was. I still think practising my reverse parking with a clear view of one of their arses in the nearside mirror was actually a decent distraction test. John would studiously ignore what was going on, even though we could both clearly hear the giggles.

Because I took the idea of passing my test so seriously, I wasn't willing to do the same to others. I wanted to feel what it was like to type that, because it's the biggest load of balls I've ever written! If I had to cope with that, then I was going to enjoy the other side – we used to hunt people down in the quiet residential streets of Henleaze and try anything to distract them. Getting in front and holding an adult magazine to the rear window was a favourite, as was generally being a nasty sod at traffic lights or screeching around roundabouts to stop them being able to join. It was like a bad episode of *The Inbetweeners* – which is ironic because during the fallout from the shitshow that was the first series of *Top Gear*, of all the abuse, and there was plenty of it, the one piece that landed hard was: 'Why is Will from *The Inbetweeners* now presenting *Top Gear*?'

I think I had ten lessons over a period of three months, then went in for a test in late April. I knew I'd failed about five minutes in. It started well enough because I could actually drive, but the nerves were terrible. I hadn't slept the night before because for all my good work in underplaying the significance of the next day, I had to acknowledge that this was The Day. Nothing else that had gone before had really mattered – exams and sports results and a decent time being bullied, all of it disappeared into a vortex of nothingness because the focus of it all had been this one day. This was the day when I'd have freedom and could spend as much time as possible behind the wheel of a car. I didn't give a fig about my A levels or having a girlfriend; I just had to pass that test.

Yep, five minutes in, on a piece of road I'd driven in every lesson with John there were some roadworks, and I fluffed something badly enough for the examiner to need to intervene. I assume these days they would just let you know you'd failed and offer you the chance to knock it on the head and skulk back to the test centre. But he made me struggle through the next 30 minutes with my nerves shattered, my back drenched in sweat and my mind completely consumed by the fallout from failing when most of my non-car-obsessed mates had breezed through their tests. I was completely broken. When we rolled into Southmead test station he chirpily announced that 'he was pleased to tell me that I had not reached the standard required by the DVLA'. What a wanker.

I tried not to go back to school – I hovered around a bit and didn't acknowledge all the kind things John Buckle said about not worrying and just getting another test booked in ASAP. This will sound quite pathetic, but the sense of otherness that day was the same as acknowledging the moments after bereavement – when you look around you and think, 'All of these people are sharing this space with me and just getting on with their lives, and they have no idea that mine has just been turned inside out, and nor should they, because that's just life.' There's a hypersensitivity to that state of mind which is a touch addictive – your senses are quite different from their normal settings, you hear things outside your normal range, the light is more brilliant, the shade darker. With all this swirling around in your head you desperately want to tell someone how shattered you are that you didn't pass your driving test. Something as pathetic as that has destabilised you to the point of uselessness. But the uncomfortable truth is that these are the people you were with a couple of days ago, wedging a copy of *Razzle* against the back window of a Nissan Micra to distract some other poor sod on his last lesson before taking a test. So there isn't going to be much sympathy.

Predictably, I phoned my mother. I was 17 and I probably cried – I can't remember. My friends absolutely crucified me, which was perfectly understandable.

The wait for the repeat test wasn't too long. It was punctuated with a couple of John lessons and a few trips out in my mother's Renault Espace. This was notable because I think the schadenfreude moment for me was the idea that I'd been prepping this Mini for months in anticipation of passing my test, and it now dawned on me how bad a look it was. I can honestly say that I never once boasted about passing first time, or suggested that I was in any way a better driver than any of my pals because I loved cars – but I'd given them all the ammo they needed to ruthlessly take the piss, and that meant I left the little red car alone. I didn't deserve to drive it until I had reached the standard required by the DVLA. What a hideous phrase that is.

Test day the second was 9 June 1992. The sun was shining, Bristol looked even more beautiful than usual – which is saying something because it is always beautiful to me. It was one of those days when everything goes right. I hardly remember the test at all, save for a perverse sense that I wish it could have continued for longer so that I could consolidate in the mind of the examiner that this time his victim really had exceeded the standard required by the DV-sodding-LA. I blagged a lift back to my parents' house after that, jumped into the Mini and drove pretty sedately around the B-roads of the Chew Valley and the Mendips. Now this was a day of pure joy – the polar opposite of what I described above. Everything possessed a super-luminescence, that muddy-red Mini was a Ferrari Rosso Corsa for the afternoon, Chew Valley Lake glimmered with a deep turquoise that no Maldivian island could hope to match. I don't think I was immature enough to ignore the significance of that day, but even allowing for me being transfixed like the Bisto kid I still didn't revere it enough. In my life there have been very few days that made me feel that good and didn't carry with them some compromise. But 9 June 1992 was flawless. Absolutely flawless.

TEN
NEW DRIVER

A driving instructor can teach you how to pass a test, but not how to drive. In the days after being granted a driving licence we are all probably reminded of this multiple times, and I was no exception. The euphoria of new-found freedom, the ecstasy of being able to drive my little Mini was tempered by the nagging fear that a nasty hill start or complicated junction could cause acute embarrassment. That was the beginning of the journey of learning to drive – 31 years later I'm still enjoying it. Some days I'm better than others, but we're always learning something because driving is perhaps the most dynamic, complicated thing we humans do on a daily basis.

These days in the UK new drivers are given the option of using a green 'P' plate to tell the world that they might be a little jumpy. And most young people are forced to fit a 'black box' to record their driving standards and use a 70mph limiter to suck the fun out of those first few months. That wasn't the case in 1992. There are many sound reasons for ensuring young drivers 'behave', but I probably wasn't thinking about them when, a few days after passing, I was pinned to the floor-boards in the Mini, downhill before the Clevedon exit of the M5, trying to nudge the tiny little speedo needle into three figures. Come on – we all did it!

Pushing it a little too far was a rite of passage for my generation. I'm not sure it's the same today. In 1992 there were a handful of speed cameras in the UK, there were far fewer cars on the roads and there was no big-brother observation network looking to nab any lane infringements. And cars could go just about anywhere. The world welcomed the car back then. The state wanted car owners to pay a road fund licence and there were police cars to give you a ticket or a ticking off, but that was all. There was a sense of freedom completely lacking for today's new drivers. Being in control of a car on your own for the first time, without the safety net of an instructor or parent to help should things go wrong, is nerve-wracking enough without the road network presenting itself as a further threat.

Today, it feels like the state doesn't just want to monitor the movement of cars, it actively wants people to trip up and infringe. For someone who's been driving for decades, it really doesn't make much of a difference beyond being a pain in the arse. If you are new to it, the sense of pressure and judgement must be appalling. There will be no statistics for the number of accidents caused by the pressure exerted by the new road environment on young people, nor how many 17-year-olds have been subjected to appalling road rage and worse because they can't clear a lane quickly due to a speed limiter, but I bet they are significant numbers. And that's before you consider the killjoy message – imagine turning 18, heading to the pub to celebrate finally being able to order a pint, only to be told you can have just the one. What a depressing way to live.

But back to 1992 – a time when a young car-obsessive could experiment with his complete lack of skill with some degree of safety. Up to a point. Life was different then, and anything I write about being a young idiot has to be viewed in context. Can you honestly remember the first time you lost control of a car? I think I can. It wasn't long after I was a free citizen, and late one Saturday night I was doing what all budding young car bores do – demonstrating how handy I was behind the wheel to a friend.

In the days before traction control and ESP and all that jazz, a Mini running a tiny tyre was quite easily unstuck. Well, that was my excuse. I can't remember exactly what happened, but a couple of thoughts did enter my head that remain with me today. The first is that when we're young and stupid we tend to ignore the bolt of fear that immediately runs down our spines the moment things go wrong. And also the comforting rush of adrenaline when, hopefully, every-thing appears to be alright.

Maybe this is the ultimate test of maturity? The imma-ture brain will style it out and, once disaster has been averted, attempt to give some impression of there never having been a problem in the first place – that everything was under control.

CHAPTER TEN

The mature brain isn't afraid to let people know that the shit very nearly hit the fan.

The second is that however light a contact might be between car and immoveable object, the resulting damage always leaves you slack-jawed. In this case it was a youthful sapling that appeared to have removed the entire side of my car without shedding a single leaf. Now this wasn't ideal, and I wasn't about to tell my parents what had happened, so I did some begging among friends and extended family and had the old girl patched up.

What I didn't do was go and learn how to control the car should the same situation arise again. And that is a bit shameful. Since my early twenties I've been genuinely curious about how to recover all sorts of driving situations that have gone wrong, but in those early days I just invoked the confidence of youth and cracked on until the next incident. Some people will read that and shudder, but that's what we did back then. Knowing what I know now, it does seem reckless, but the world was a different place and that was that.

Lift-off oversteer was a very real thing too. Mine wasn't the generation of the Mk2 Escort and cosy stories of learning to slide on cross-plies and cobbled streets. I'm younger than that. Only one of my friends had a rear-wheel drive car; it was a Morris Traveller bought for him by his father, and he hated the bloody thing. We were all front-driven. That should have meant immunity from on-road spins and off-road excursions, but there's a strong argument to suggest that the front-driven cars of the late eighties and early nineties were some of the most difficult machines to handle.

If you don't know what oversteer is, it's a miracle you've persevered with the book to this point, so I'll leave you to google it. Or have my ultimate driving hero, Walter Röhrl, explain: 'When you see the tree you're driving into you have understeer, when you hear it you have oversteer.'

An old-fashioned rear-wheel drive car tends to slide because there is too much power for the grip available. The classic scenario is a wet road surface and someone driving away from a T-junction and – whoops – suddenly they're facing the wrong way. The key here is it happens at relatively low speed.

Front-wheel drive cars can't push themselves into a low-speed spin because the front wheels are dragging the car along – but this brings with it the nasty bastard that is lift-off oversteer. This happens, wet-and-dry, when you enter a corner too fast and think 'cripes, I'd better back off a bit here' and then the rear axle decides to overtake the front wheels. Couple of things to note: this tends to happen at much higher speed than the rear-drive version, and, because no one ever teaches us how to collect a slide like this, almost all instances end in some kind of shunt as the car slaps from one side to the other and the driver looks like they're trying to punch themselves in the face.

Quite how I didn't smash my first Peugeot 205 to pieces still remains a potential reason for finding Godot, but I did have a spin that went well beyond the 360-degree mark. All Bristolians will know the off-ramp that links the flyover with the Portway, a nasty off-camber left hander, and it was there that I thought to myself, 'I'm going a bit quick here, I'll just back off a little and whoooooooaaaaaaaahhhh, shiiiiiiiiiiiit.' I still drive down there and wonder how I missed all the hard metal and concrete bits.

I've always blamed myself for that incident, which is mostly correct, save for the bit about French cars. Now I'd always read about French front-wheel drive cars being a bit more lively in this respect, but the reality was shocking. If you drove a Ford Fiesta, it just wouldn't land you in the same trouble, nor a Golf. Both of those cars had chassis whose priority was to not allow lift-off oversteer. That was the starting point for most of them – don't let people get into strife when they want to adjust their speed mid-corner. The French had a completely different philosophy: make small hatchbacks as much fun to drive as possible.

It really was a crazy time to be driving because there is no way on earth it would be allowed to happen today. The core conflict of front-wheel drive is that for it to be fun the car has to be a little bit edgy and, dare I say it, dangerous. It has to be susceptible to lift-off oversteer. That's what makes the steering sharp and the car want to tighten its line when you make small adjustments to the throttle. So what I'm actually saying is that French hatchbacks from the eighties and early nineties are in fact a metaphor for adult life – anything that is great fun probably carries with it some element of risk.

The other mad thing about that period in time, one in which surely every insurance company knew that a French hatchback was much more likely to spear through a hedgerow than one made in any other country, is that there has always been a way of dealing with most extreme lift-off situations. Just bury the throttle. It sounds quite ridiculous, and it's certainly counterintuitive, but it works! The trouble is, no one ever teaches us this stuff as an 'ordinary' driver. You need to digest the stopping distances of a Ford Anglia and how many stowaways you can find in a 40-tonne truck, but not how to avoid the most common, self-inflicted accident of them all.

It's probably not acceptable to satirise my own hapless forays into driving and then decry the lack of basic training given to all drivers. But I do find it seriously odd that most people have spent far more time being coached how to hit a tennis ball or kick a football than how to control a motor car when things go wrong. There is a direct comparison with sex education in the UK. I know, very icky, but bear with me. Back in the eighties it really was a one-hour lecture where most people were laughing or exchanging Garbage Pail Kids cards, and some home learning around the back of the bike sheds. The same went for driving: teach yourself. Nowadays kids are almost overloaded with information on the physical side of relationships, to the point of technique being a thing! And driving? Slightly longer theory test, otherwise still the same. I still think it's madness that the most dangerous thing most people will do on a daily basis requires no basic skills training beyond the silly test.

Anyhow, back to some double-standard stories of me behaving like a pillock back in the day. There is a very good reason why none of my kids will have a Mini as their first car – I'm not sure how I survived in mine. I drove it absolutely flat-to-the-boards everywhere – that little Mountney steering wheel wriggling around and the two Corbeau bucket seats I'd fitted flexing in ways that make me cringe sitting here now. It was so much fun. And ridiculously dangerous.

Somerset is a county of lanes and high hedges. And anyone who lives there knows that this means the most fun is to be had after dark. Even the committed young lunatic of limited intelligence works out that in the daytime you drive blind, in the night-time you can see headlights coming towards you. This left you with a couple of potential issues. First, people walking or, more commonly, driving back from the pub. The landlord of one local used to give his most inebriated customers a deadly stare and say, 'You're too drunk to walk, make sure you drive home.' That reads appallingly now, but the most common accident back then was some old soak wobbling about in the lanes and being collected by a late-commuting BMW. Hence the landlord's advice.

The other was the local copper. These were the last days of the village policeman, and ours was a good'un. He knew the ways of the world and would occasionally lurk in his police van to see who was behaving badly after dark. That was often me. I'm mostly a law-abiding citizen, but being followed by a copper when you hadn't really done much wrong quickly became good sport – especially once you realised just how slow a three-door diesel Escort Estate police car was. Imagine the sheer misery of using that to catch some little twerp in a

Mini. This was a low-powered Somerset version of *The Dukes of Hazzard*, with one posh voice, several Wurzel-sounding people and no Daisy. It wouldn't make good telly. But they were happy days, and apart from launching the Mini through the odd hedge and having to beg the farmer to tow it back out the next morning, no harm was done. I'm not sure what a black box would have made of any of it.

Not long after that came the first experience of looking for a parked car and being quite baffled as to why it wasn't where it should have been. I looked down the next road and wasn't remotely worried until it dawned on me – cue the most awful tummy ker-klunk – that someone has stolen my car. My pride and joy. Many of us have experienced it and, if you love cars, it's not easy to explain to other people that the hurt goes beyond the loss of a material object.

Factor in this being your first car and one which you've been lavishing so much time and effort on, and the fallout is shattering. Acknowledge the locked-in passion you have for cars and in particular your own car, and – with literally no one save perhaps your mother knowing how badly this might affect you – it's all a bit sad. Many of you will have been in the same position. Isn't it strange that of all the things I might wish on people I don't much like, one isn't having a car stolen. That's off the books. Waterboarding, absolutely fine, but hands off their motor car.

They found it, on its roof, shorn of all the decent extra bits I'd added, mostly burnt-out, on a playing field in a rough part of town. It was recovered to a garage in Clifton and I went down to see it. What a crappy experience that was, walking into a dingy workshop and seeing the scorched, twisted remains of the thing I'd put so much love into. The insurance money was a pittance – I hadn't listed any of the modifications because they wouldn't have been allowed.

I think this was the first time in my life that I slightly fell out of love with cars. It was A-level summer and the sun was shining and there was the pub and I was playing cricket every other day and, you know what, for the first time life was just fine without cars. Once bitten, twice shy. Isn't it utterly ridiculous that my first experience of emotionally overcommitting to something and then being a bit broken when it went wrong wasn't anything to do with a girl, it was all down to a Mini City? What a weirdo, even if I do say so myself.

The car that came next confirmed a drift away from the world only being about cars. The aforementioned lift-off oversteering, bog-standard Peugeot 205 1.1, pre-facelift 5dr in red. Nothing remotely sporty, but in reality one of the most comfortable cars I've ever driven. It was bought instead of a Mini Metro that was cheaper but whose rear quarter panel had one of the worst repairs I've seen to this day. But it looked too cheap to ignore. The deal fell through when I drove it and a large part of that panel fell out, revealing some comically poor filler work. And the padding behind it? A scrunched-up copy of the *Bristol Evening Post*, dated a few weeks earlier. So, the Peugeot it was.

ELEVEN
UNIVERSITY
(POLYTECHNIC)

After flunking my A levels I spent several months lurking around Bristol pretending to have a clue what I wanted to do with the rest of my life. I bought and sold a few cars, flogged dodgy car warranties, packed envelopes for a while and then went off to Africa to teach in a school. At the time it just felt like I'd gone and done something mildly interesting for a while and then returned to the UK. Thinking back, teaching in a state boarding school in Zimbabwe probably had a greater effect on me than I realised at the time.

I flew to Harare on 8 May 1994. You'll notice there are very few exact dates in this book, but I remember this one for two reasons. The first is still difficult to write about – the death of Ayrton Senna. The second is the McLaren F1.

For someone my age with a passion for cars or motorsport, Senna's death during the San Marino Grand Prix at Imola on

1 May 1994 was a moon-landing moment. You know exactly where you were when it happened. I was at Chew Stoke with my parents. It was a blazing hot day and my mother was lizarding in the garden and my father was indulging in his favourite retirement activity – tending to his tomatoes.

We all know what happened that day: the start-line crash, the safety car (which I always remember was an Opel Vectra 4x4) and then the awful crash that claimed Senna's life. He was my hero racing driver at the time despite me being a massive Nigel Mansell fan. Nigel had left F1 to go to America in 1993, and since then, like so many millions of other F1 fans, I'd fallen under the spell of the brooding Brazilian. I can remember watching the footage in disbelief. Those of you who saw it might remember an overhead shot from a helicopter that clearly showed Senna's head move in the cockpit. I remember allowing myself to use this as a way of clinging to some hope that he was alive. A few hours later the BBC cut to a broadcast from Murray Walker, away from the circuit, announcing that Senna had died. I just sat watching the television and cried.

Senna had been one of those permanents in my life. Not a week went by when I didn't see him on television or read something about him. He was superhuman. He had assumed a status above all other drivers – that of a living legend – and this was unusual for someone still competing at the top level. Normally such plaudits are only bestowed on people who have retired or passed away. Because of this, even accepting the awful reality that just one day earlier Roland

Ratzenberger had perished in qualifying, Senna had seemed immortal. The sport hadn't had a fatality for years, but in the space of one weekend in Emilia-Romagna that comfortable status quo was shattered.

I wish I'd jumped into my car and headed into Bristol after seeing Murray hold back his tears on live television, because I somehow ended up having a huge row with my dad. He asked me to do something, and I probably suggested that it could wait given that Senna had just died and I was a little cut up about it. He never liked cars and wasn't remotely interested in racing, but his insensitivity to me being upset didn't sit well – if it had been a cricket player my emotional state would probably have been acceptable – so we exchanged words.

A week later I set off for Zimbabwe, still with some bad blood lingering between me and my father. Before he passed away, I had only seen my mother cry once, and that was dropping me off at Bristol Airport to go on that big adventure. Lately I've scrutinised whether it actually was a big adventure, and you know what? It was.

How the hell I managed to leave the UK three days before the publication of the one issue of a car magazine I'd been waiting for I will never know – but it happened. The *Autocar* road test of the McLaren F1, complete with a full set of performance figures which I still think, in the context of what was considered fast at the time, are the most extraordinary bunch of numbers extracted from a street car. It wasn't until I worked at *Autocar* that I finally managed to bag a copy of that magazine, dated 11 May 1994.

I flew on a strange semi-cargo/passenger KLM 747 via Johannesburg, was collected at Harare airport by a total stranger, and after a night at some prep school, jumped on a school bus to a place called Plumtree. From that moment on I had a new meaning for the phrase 'the middle of nowhere'. Google it and you'll find a place that is 60 miles west of Bulawayo, on the edge of the Kalahari Desert and the Highveld bordering South Africa. I arrived, met the headmaster and was shown to my rondavel – a mud-hut with a thatched roof. I was there to coach hockey and generally help out.

It was one of the most rewarding times of my life. Now, I love a decent Gap Yaaaar Instagram clip as much as the next privileged public-school tosser, but the irrefutable truth is that back in the early nineties there were no mobile phones, no internet, no real means of communicating apart from written letters and the occasional telephone call that cost a fortune. Yes, I'd been at boarding school for a while, but in Africa I really was on my own. I'd been given £100 cash, had no credit card and was told to get on with it!

Within a few weeks I was teaching English too, and had been invited to join the local cricket club. This meant hitching into Bulawayo in the back of a bakkie and then playing at other schools or random pitches on huge farms. The kids were a revelation – funny, intelligent and hard as nails. If you ever find yourself facing up to someone who went to one of those schools, then walk away. They played rugby on compacted mud that was as hard as concrete. One boy, who can't have been much more than 12 years old, was bitten by a puff adder

How not to dress a child.
Crantock 1980ish.

Happy times in the pool at home.

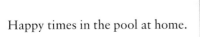

Father, mother, brother Paul and
myself. We don't look alike.

Rare image of me not arguing
with my father in the early
1990s. We fixed that, luckily.

Early brand work for the
Sony Naked Walkman.

Visiting Tamiya UK –
kid in a sweet shop.

My crash helmet still
reminds me of those
happy times.

Clifton College in Bristol. Doesn't look like *Grange Hill*.

Forgot games kit for team photo day.

Last day of school, 1993. I loved my time there.

Plumtree School,
Zimbabwe 1994. They
played rugby on that.

West Glos Hockey
Club, Amsterdam.
Hockey and cars
were everything.

About all I can
remember from
Oxford Brookes.

The great LJK was
always deciding.

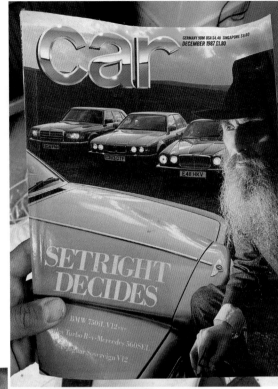

Letter to *Performance Car*
1993 defending J. Clarkson.

print all the letters, but
here are a few...

MISSING THE POINT

Well done, Mr Morris of
Walton-on-the-Hill. I hope that
your spleen is now well and
truly vented. Your vituperative
and vitriolic attack on
Clarkson proves nothing
more than your total failure to
understand what he
represented or tried to
achieve.

That *Performance Car* is a
great monthly read and
terrific value for money, few
would dispute. Its reporting,
testing, accuracy and
presentation are beyond
reproach. Furthermore, it
reports on cars that I *want* to
learn about, whether I can
afford them or not.

At the end of all this quality
presentation, Clarkson made
his contribution. He brought
us down to earth, more often
than not with the finesse and
subtlety of an Exocet. He
played the devil's advocate,
shocked, annoyed,
questioned and made us
think for ourselves. All this
with a sense of humour.

If he annoyed you, Mr
Morris, why did you read his
column? There were 160
other pages you could have
read.
**Gareth Jones,
Carmarthen**

OUTSTANDING CHARACTERS

● *Clarkson gave us plenty of laughs, as John
Barker demonstrates. It'll be quiet around here*

my favourites — the layout is
uncompromised by
advertising and the road
testers seem to be unique
among automotive journalists
because they are very real
characters. Through their
reactions to particular cars
and the way in which they
assess attributes, and more
importantly through the feel
they get from just being in
contact with certain
machinery, I can derive a
picture of the character that is
writing the article. This sets
PC apart from all other
magazines.

As normal I bought it on
publication day, began at the
front and worked through. It
was superb — I loved it all
and agreed with almost
everything (apart from the
Alfa beating the 530i!). Then
came Clarkson's bombshell.

obstinate and immune to
criticism chucks in the towel
because of the rantings of
some Joe Bloggs then what
hope is there for us young
hopefuls? The suppression of
a character like Clarkson is
identical to the loss of
adventurous car designers —
as he said himself recently,
cars are becoming blander.
For God's sake don't let
journalism go the same way.
It's a sad day.
**Christopher Harris,
Bristol**

TEN YEARS OF GOOD READING

It is with great disappointment
that the first time I have ever
written to a magazine is to say
how I couldn't seem to enjoy
reading it, despite its usual

LEFT FE[...] FLAT

Sunday afterno[...]
down to relax b[...]
Performance C[...]
the last page a[...]
column. Next s[...]
Plant Hire to re[...]
steam-roller. C[...]
me how long it [...]
drive from Som[...]
Walton-the-[...]
the maximum s[...]
transport is 6m[...]

I am very so[...]
Clarkson will n[...]
contributing to [...]
excellent maga[...]
often smiled to [...]
complaining le[...]
appear and be[...]
Clarkson has g[...]
alternative and [...]
aspect to both [...]
everyday issue[...]
if you ever war[...]
a steam-roller.[...]
**Simon Pear[...]
Bridgwater**

MR MO[...] SORRY [...]

Well I never ex[...]
pleasure of be[...]
the namedrop[...]
Clarkson's Pe[...]
column. As he[...]
suggested, it i[...]
fault that he ha[...]
magazine and [...]
accepting tha[...]

21 Savannah, not embedded in a tree.

One of my father's Audis – a 90 Quattro.

Mini City.
My first car.

106 XSI that replaced
a 205 XS. Poor swap.

306 XSI in France.
Fantastic car.

Elise caked in flies
after non-stop
dash to south of
France, 1998.

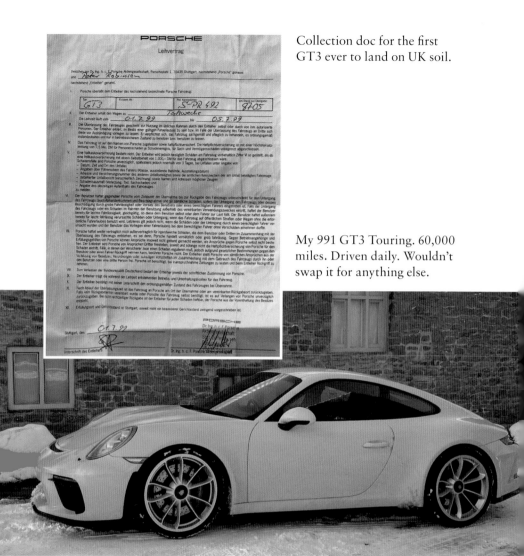

Collection doc for the first GT3 ever to land on UK soil.

My 991 GT3 Touring. 60,000 miles. Driven daily. Wouldn't swap it for anything else.

E199 NOT up on three wheels, as usual. 911 CS, my first 911. 2000.

right outside my hut one morning on his way to morning chapel. He was back in lessons after lunch, minus the finger.

And they were extraordinary athletes – the school sits 4,500ft above sea level, so they spent most of their time inadvertently altitude training for life. I've never really been that serious about fitness, normally finding the bare minimum to do what was needed to race a car or play hockey, but that was the only time I became properly fit and lost a load of weight.

Zimbabwe was already far more politically complicated than a sheltered 19-year-old would understand. Robert Mugabe had been in power for more than a decade, but the economy was just beginning to slide and its heavy reliance on South Africa wasn't sustainable. But what I initially found was a government-funded boarding school with 50 per cent white kids and the other half black or mixed-race (or 'goffel', as they called us) that co-existed well and produced inquisitive, clever pupils who, as mentioned above, you should avoid at all costs in a fighting situation.

It turns out there was rather more going on. Towards the end of my time there – as the Zimbabwean dollar began to tank and I realised corporal punishment was freely allowed and the headmaster was using his full allowance, and the surface racial harmony might have a bubbling undercurrent – I went off to get my visa extended. Because despite the above, I rather liked working there. Only when the chap behind the desk at Beitbridge border post took my passport and left to head into some back room did things seem a little odd. He returned stern-faced and started telling me I was working illegally and that he was keeping my passport so that the authorities could put me on a train and deport me within 48 hours. This was a little scary. The only upside being that the angry shouty man wasn't very good at remembering where he had put things – namely, my passport – which he'd left on the counter, and he tried to grab it a second after I'd stuffed it into my pocket and run out of the door. The trip back was completed briskly in a borrowed Honda Accord.

I did leave the country within 48 hours. I ended up in a place called Mahalapye, Botswana – which made Plumtree look like New York, and I spent a few days with a family whose seven-year-old was an absolute demon at finding scorpions. And then I went up to the north of Botswana, took some terrible photographs, and wandered back into Zimbabwe through the Victoria Falls border. The joys of pre-computerised border controls.

This was a period of non-driving, and that of course meant watching others drive. Something car people tend to be very bad at. The roads in Africa were at times very beautiful and also very shocking. I saw things there that I wouldn't want to write about and have tried to forget, but they are just part of the process of seeing more of the world, and perhaps realising how well ordered and safe our west-ernised lives are. The two car memories that will always endure are borrowing a friend's Peugeot 504 and driving to the far east of Zimbabwe. A formidably tough machine and easily a match for anything Mercedes has built. The other was being charged by a white rhino in the Matobo

National Park while being driven in a rented Talbot Horizon by a school pal who wasn't especially gifted. That did get my attention.

It was around this time that I received a telegram, or telefax, or something that was a bit weird and I thought I'd once seen in a Bond film, from my father, congratulating me on being accepted into Oxford Polytechnic.

This struck me as unusual because since deciding not to accept Aberystwyth on its generous 2-E offer (the only offer I received after getting an A and two Ds at A level) I hadn't applied for any further education places. I was in fact priming myself to announce to my father on my return from my African adventure that I didn't want to go to polytechnic – instead I was going to sell cars.

A month later I was back in Somerset, standing in my father's study. He was telling me that Oxford Polytechnic was about to become Oxford Brookes University and that he had secured a place for me while I was away. I told him, respectfully, that I didn't see any value in higher education and that I wanted to get out into the real world and make my way. Africa had taught me that students were decadent and lazy and they told shit stories, and I wanted no part of it.

'I'll pay your rent and give you £400 a month to spend on beer,' he said.

'I've always wanted to be a student,' I replied. 'When does term start?'

Another early lesson in life – always accept a bribe if the money is good enough.

CHAPTER ELEVEN

So having temporarily shelved my need to join the honest workforce of the UK, I headed off to the gleaming spires of Oxford Brookes, which had just gained university status.

An early hiccup was overcome when I appeared at the psychology faculty only to be told that my name wasn't on the list. Back at the main campus someone helpful told me that I had been enrolled to do English and book publishing, not English and psychology – and given that changing it would probably mean missing an agreed pub appointment with some school pals I made the agonising decision to go with book publishing. Even though beyond the obvious title I had literally no idea what it was about. A few weeks later my father did admit that he was having a few issues with his handwriting and could have written PB (publishing), rather than PS (psychology), but by then neither of us really cared because I'd made it into the 1st XI hockey team. Yep, those hard yards in Africa had made me even more of an entitled sod.

The first year at Brookes was a little bit tricky because I didn't make it into halls of residence and had to blag a room with a load of final-year students. They were mostly girls and they looked after me, but I didn't really meet many people outside of the hockey club and I used to head back to Bristol at weekends to see my girlfriend.

All of those Oxford–Bristol dashes were undertaken in what remains one of the best cars I've ever owned – the 1988 Peugeot 205 XS. I still crap on about how great these little cheese-boxes were, but back then the XS was a revelation to me. It had 85hp from a 1360cc motor, the best five-speed gearbox I've ever used and its little 165 section tyres gave enough grip for it to scoot about but enough sidewall to be comfy as hell. Bung in the sexy bolstered seats from the GTi and you had the perfect small hatchback. There were many ways of describing just how special the XS was. Some said it was a cut-price GTi with better steering and a more exciting engine. Others suggested it was an insurance bargain. Remember, this was the time when car insurance costs went through the roof and anyone under the age of 25 faced huge costs. But the little XS was group 8, whereas a GTi was group 15.

But what they all wanted to say, including me, was this: if you drove an XS like a twat, it was probably quicker than some ponce who couldn't really drive in a 1.6 GTi. I've always wanted to type that.

I loved that car – adored the way the Solex carb had twin chokes so you could feel an extra resistance to the pedal as the extra power was released. I was living a happy life then – I had a fantastic group of school friends and we'd all managed to stay in touch despite moving all over the country. Brookes was fun and I had a girlfriend, but the thing I could probably never admit at the time was being at my happiest behind the wheel of a six-year-old Peugeot.

And so, beginning a trend that continues to this day, I managed to bollocks that up completely by selling a great car and buying a less good car. The XS was chopped in for a 106 XSi, which was slower, less fun to drive and I didn't really enjoy. But it looked cool, had a decent bass tube in the boot and an Oakley sticker on the rear screen, so all was well. I also didn't lose a penny when I sold it, which was not a trend that I managed to continue much in later life.

The second year at uni was exceptional. It had it all – I lived with a large Welshman from school, a lunatic Italian who knew his cars and the closest physical match to Hagrid from *Harry Potter* I've ever seen. We lived the student dream – rented the most disgusting property I've ever set foot in, drank ourselves stupid and played computer games.

Initially we were the only student slum on the road to not be robbed – a white van would roll down these known non-civilian roads off the Cowley Road, as a couple of scary-looking dudes knocked on doors and politely suggested you hand over valuables. We were slumped on the hideous, sticky sofas one afternoon when there was a knock at the door – Hagrid, or Geoff as he was called, went to open it. He came back in saying there was a dodgy-looking bloke asking to borrow a screwdriver. 'Tell him to fuck off,' we said, which Geoff duly did. The crim was so staggered by the sheer size of him – 6ft 6in and 20 stone – that he thought better of it and tried next door. Of course they came back a few days later when we were out and stripped the place.

If there has been no mention of academic activity up to this point, there's good reason. I didn't really do any. The English faculty was completely baffling to me. I'd come from a traditional teaching background and was presented with the absolute forefront of what would now be called a 'woke' institution. The first lecture I sat in I was told it was unreasonable to use the pronouns he or she, and that only the dual construct of 'shahe' was acceptable. In 1994, this completely blew my mind. But the sad fact is the English faculty at Brookes was actually very good and full of bright people I could have learnt from, but I didn't really engage and I regret that enormously.

The only lecture I can remember was given by a small Scottish chap called Archie Burnett. The subject was Shakespeare's *The Taming of the Shrew*. He stood up, waited for quiet and said: '*The Taming of the Shrew*, or is it the Shaming of the True?' That's stupendously clever, but rather than absorb the knowledge of people who were experts in the subject that I found fascinating and explore in a way that I must have known would nourish my brain and make me a better person, I pretended to like football, learnt the words to 'Three Lions' and spent the majority of the summer of 1996 on the piss. Therein probably lies the prerogative of all middle-class university students throughout time: almost be seduced by doing something sensible, but actually just get drunk.

What a summer it was, though. The sun shone every day, I had a top group of friends, and, in a rare moment of mature thinking, I wrote a letter to *Autocar* magazine asking if I might come and do some work experience. A couple of weeks later they replied offering me a stint in the summer holidays.

Now this was perfect timing. As we all know, life really is about luck and timing; the rest is just window dressing. I was an utterly lazy young man who did nothing but arse around, but I did read car magazines. And by that, I mean I read *Autocar* every week; *Car Magazine*, *Performance Car*, *Max Power* – all of them were devoured. The Italian lunatic was a part of this too, as he loved his cars and was probably the first person in a social situation I had the opportunity to chat with about the subject I was most passionate and knew the most about. As a parent now, I really don't want my kids to have a locked-in passion for something and feel unable to express it until they are 21 years old. It probably isn't healthy and might go some way to explaining some of the bad decisions I made during those years.

Never mind – I had a chance to go and meet the people I'd been reading for years. The people who had lived inside my head.

TWELVE
WORK
EXPERIENCE

A friend let me sleep on his floor in central London and I drove down to the *Autocar* office in Teddington. You could still just about do that in 1996 without a camera snapping you and charging you to drive on the roads that you've already paid for twice. I left at 6am to be there for 9am – which is ridiculous – but outside of taking my driving test, this was the most important day of my life. At the time I didn't know why, but the fact I'd managed to get up, shave, iron a shirt and generally join the human race must have been evidence enough. Regardless of whether this would be life-changing or not, I was desperately excited to meet the names I'd been reading for years, not considering for one minute how they might react to me.

I drove in glorious sunshine, with very little traffic on the roads. 'Good Enough' by Dodgy was playing on Chris Evans's

Radio 1 Breakfast Show – oh, the irony – and I rolled into TW12 about two hours early. The office was on Hampton Road and there was a bus stop opposite. I parked my car, grabbed a takeaway cup of tea and then sat there watching people arrive for work. The first was Steve Cropley. He sneaked into the car park in a BMW 728i – the E38 model and still the prettiest 7 Series ever made.

Now Steve won't mind me saying this, but in the pantheon of celebrities likely to have bystanders point and say to the total stranger next to them, 'Look its so-and-so!' he probably doesn't sit high on most lists. But for the 21-year-old me, he was absolute box-office and I couldn't quite believe my eyes when he shuffled into the office. Other staff members arrived and, again, they triggered in me a need to tell complete strangers (don't worry, I resisted) waiting to take the bus to Twickenham that the Consumer Editor for *Autocar* magazine had just arrived in a new Renault Scenic! A bloody Scenic – the one with the storage bin under the rear seats! After an hour of weirdo lurking, I plucked up the courage to go inside.

Since that day I've had the chance to jangle my nerves before meeting many famous, powerful people, but none of it compares to August 1996. The editor was called Michael Harvey. He didn't pay me much attention because he had a magazine to make, but his deputy, Mark Harrop, did. He gave me something menial to do – check all the papers for a decent automotive story or something similar – and I tried to concentrate on the task but just couldn't help but look around and grin at what was around me.

We spend a lot of time complaining about social media and the evils it propagates in society, but we rarely mention the upsides. Young people can now express their quirky interests without fear of judgement – in fact they can use what would once have been condemned as downright strange to become internet sensations. Just look at Francis Bourgeois, the chap who whoops and screeches as trains whizz past him. The only differences between him now and me aged 21 in that situation was I didn't have an outlet to demonstrate my strange obsession with this office of ordinary people producing a magazine about cars, and I didn't have one of those odd 360-degree cameras that leaves him looking like Sid from *Ice Age*. If I'd been allowed both of those things I'd have celebrated seeing Steve Sutcliffe arrive with a special flourish and jumped up and down like a five-year-old.

A couple of days in I was allowed to go to Millbrook with Steve to test the new Jaguar XK8. This was probably the day that cemented what I wanted to do with the rest of my life. Millbrook is one of two industry test centres in the UK where carmakers develop their new models. Back then it was owned by GM and it had the only high-speed bowl in the country – a place where you could do well over 150mph in a constant circle. The mile-straight that was used by car magazines to extract performance data ran alongside it.

These days you can accurately time any car by using a cheap app and fixing your iPhone to the dashboard. It was a little more complicated back then and involved a heavy sensor you bolted to the side of the car which was attached to a laptop operated by the passenger. It was probably £10,000 worth of kit, and it didn't always work. Performance figures were at the very heart of car-magazine culture back then – the first thing people like me did was head to the data section of a road test, or a group test, and see how machinery fared against the clock. Today people watch drag races on YouTube, but they're really the same thing, answering that very basic human curiosity around what's fastest. It doesn't matter if it's dropping sticks into a river, or watching athletes at a track, or 2,500hp top-fuel dragsters shooting flames, we just want to know what is the quickest.

I sat there for an afternoon as Steve ran through all the acceleration runs and then the in-gear pulls and then on to the banking, which felt pretty uncomfortable at 155mph. None of that mattered because it was, frankly, a dream come true. Most people or activities we've built-up an expectation for tend to be a crashing disappointment, but not this. In my oddball pre-influencer, locked-in-weirdo world I had probably pictured what it would be like to go and test a car at Millbrook, and the reality was even better.

Before we left the track, Steve pulled a huge slide between two metal gate posts, drifted most of a lap of what was called the 'Hill Route' and then sauntered home. Viv Richards, Nigel Mansell, Ayrton Senna – and now Steve Sutcliffe. I had a new hero.

The way he drove the car was mesmerising to me. Until that point, I thought I could drive a bit – but the car control, the slides and the accuracy made me realise I wasn't even in the same universe as him. He sat in the car differently – more upright and with the wheel closer to his hands because that was the only way he could control it so closely and with such accuracy. That evening I moved the backrest of my Peugeot 306 into a more vertical position and made sure I could lay both of my wrists on the steering wheel with some bend in my arms. I've sat like that in every car, ever since. And if you can recall a stranger coming-of-age scenario than that, I'll happily buy you a pint.

The logical upshot of this day with Steve was that I now wanted to be a road tester so desperately that failing at university presented very little appeal, so I decided that on the last day of my work experience I would ask Mark if there might be a job of any sort on the horizon. This was nixed when, on the morning I was going to ask, there was a right old kerfuffle in the office, and when I plucked up the courage to ask what was happening, someone said, 'Michael Harvey has left the building.'

I said my goodbyes and assumed that within the turmoil of their boss being asked to leave the building, any chance of coming to the *Autocar* office again was unlikely. In those days you didn't exchange mobile phone numbers or leave a DM on Facebook or Instagram, you just left and realised that the only way contact between you and that person or organisation would occur again was if you made it happen. That's fundamentally different from the way things are now. It would mean writing a letter or making a telephone call, and that would mean being a total pain in the arse. Which is another life lesson I learnt far too late. Most people who get somewhere have been a total pain in the arse in pursuing someone or something, and if at times this reads like a shit version of the moral ending to an episode of *He-Man* then I'm only partly apologetic.

I went back to Oxford Brookes utterly convinced that I knew what I wanted to do, and equally convinced that there was no way to achieve it. An emotionally confusing situation that, in hindsight, probably explains some of the shitshow that was the next year. Self-destruction is one of my stronger skills, and so I became a little more rogue and landed myself in ever sillier situations that culminated in me punching one of those reinforced panes of glass. The ones with the metal in them. I'd had a few sherbets and stormed out of a pub.

Once the door closed behind me I looked at my arm and there was blood spurting from my wrist. I hadn't seen that before. It was quite mesmerising the way it spurted and landed on the pavement, and also a little worrying. When you've made the dramatic 'fuck you, I'm leaving' gesture, then punched a window and stormed out, the last thing you want to do is walk back into that pub and ask the people you've just told to fuck off to help you. But that's what I had to do, and that's probably how I became friends with a chap called Richard Tuthill.

He was in the hockey club with me and a good driver. I was losing quite a lot of blood, so him and a few others – I genuinely can't remember who – bundled me into his clapped-out Golf to the local hospital. The last thing I remember was him executing a perfect handbrake turn the wrong way around Magdalen roundabout and thinking that this was the only piece of driving I'd experienced that was as impressive as Steve Sutcliffe in a Jag. Shortly after that I must have passed out.

Self-inflicted injuries like that are especially pathetic and wasteful, so I need to apologise to anyone who had to patch me up that night. There was all sorts of nerve damage and the thing started to smell a bit lively, so the next week I was at Frenchay Hospital in Bristol having an operation and being told to not be a knob in future. But I did do a proper job on my right wrist and hand. Driving was off the cards for quite a while and this probably pitched me into an even worse place, and that's when I ended up doing far too much of everything and having what the medical profession would call an 'episode'.

I don't really know what happened, but one morning I couldn't breathe and then I must have passed out, and when I came to I didn't feel very well at all. I went through a series of tests, all of which concluded that I didn't have epilepsy, I'd just been even more of a knob than when I'd punched a window. The problem here being that any doctor who has a patient that presents as having suffered a loss of consciousness is obliged to inform the DVLA of the episode, and that results in an immediate suspension of their driving licence for a minimum of 12 months.

I underwent loads more tests to prove to the DVLA that it was a one-off, but to no avail. As you can probably imagine, in the context of what I've written above, this wasn't a very good place for me to be. It left me completely desolate and I didn't know how to drag myself out of that dark place. It was the first time in my life I'd been unable to sleep and, worse still, it drew out of me nervous clinches and ticks that made me concerned that I *did* have something more sinister wrong with me. I went to the doctor and he gave me a prescription for something called carbamazepine. It's not very pleasant stuff and it made me feel like dog poo for many months – and I now know that there was absolutely no reason for me to take it at the time.

Carbamazepine did have one unexpected positive side-effect, though. Throughout this time I lived with the same idiots and hung out with the same goons from the sports club, despite the fact that I was no longer allowed to drink on the pills. This fall from grace was greeted with just the right amount of care and ruthless piss-taking, given that I'd been central to most of the drinking activities before pushing things a little too far.

The upside was the brand name of the drug itself. I'd been totally honest with my pals about what had happened and what I was taking. It was called Tegretol. Because it was supposed to release slowly, some sadistic bastard in the 'drug-naming department' had decided to add the word 'Retard'. Tegretol Retard. Imagine being 22 years old and faced with a bunch of merciless mates after doing the funky chicken, and then taking pills called Retard? They had a field day. In fact, they still do, despite me not swallowing one of those bloody things since 1999.

That summer was supposed to have been my second stint doing work experience at *Autocar*. I'd sent the letter, and they had replied saying they were looking forward to having me back (I cannot tell you how good that made me feel over a simple 'you can come on this date') – but now I didn't have a driving licence. Even by my standards of creating shitshows, this was special.

There weren't many options, but all of them were apocalyptic to me. Anything that shakes a 22-year-old who has led a largely trauma-free life makes them feel like the world is going to end. I decided the best thing to do was phone the new editor, Patrick Fuller, and tell him that I was no longer able to come and do my two-week stint, and to be honest about why that was the case. He paused, then told me to come anyway. That was a kind and pivotal gesture.

My old, retired and now very confused father said he'd drive me to London one evening in August, so that I could do work experience at a car magazine without the ability to drive a car on the public highway. We never spoke about it afterwards but I have to assume that he was merely doing what all decent parents do – supporting the obvious madness of a child because there doesn't seem much else you can do at the time. Kind man.

All I remember about that second stint at *Autocar* was Colin Goodwin ending up on the grass at Thruxton in a 106 GTi and getting so much air inside the cabin it looked like his head was going to punch a hole in the roof.

After that I went back to Brookes to begin my fourth year of a three-year course. Yes, I had completely flunked the previous year. A few off-games notes might have been possible in light of the poor behaviour, but I had to go back and try to finish the course. That didn't go especially well, but it did give me an excellent working knowledge of all the train and bus services in Bristol and Oxford. It also introduced me to the joys of the 'permit to travel' and hiding in train toilets as the ticket inspector wandered through.

Oxford Brookes no longer required me after Christmas 1997, so I went back to Bristol to live with my girlfriend and generally sulk. No driving licence, no prospects and everyone else I knew graduating or being offered jobs they fully deserved because they had worked hard and not done what I had done. Pretty bleak times. I wrote to Patrick Fuller again and he very kindly offered me a few days at *Autocar* and then a few days at *Classic & Sports Car*, but these were a kind concession for a sad young man who clearly wasn't going to make the grade.

In February 1998, the last time I did work experience with Haymarket, who owned all these car magazines, I asked Patrick if I could have a few minutes with him. I asked him what chance there was of a job when I did have a driving licence. Fair play to him, he eyeballed me and said that even with a permit to drive I was probably a bit too much of a liability, but he recognised my strange knowledge of all things cars and my enthusiasm. He said I should stay in contact but his advice was to look for other jobs. I smiled, thanked him for giving me a chance, went outside and tried very hard not to cry.

The next few months were a bit of a blur. The day my licence was restored it was snowing, so I drove my girlfriend's Citroën AX GT like a prick and then settled back into the normal routine which involved playing a new video game called *Gran Turismo*. Without that game I really would have been in trouble. But I had zero prospects and was also about to butt up against an uncomfortable reality check that might make some of what you've been reading make a bit more sense.

My dear, kind father adopted me into a life of frankly unimaginable prosperity and kindness, considering what might have happened to me. Occasionally I would do a holiday job, but when I was 15 he told me not to bother with earning money like that. He said I'd have to spend the rest of my life working, so while he was looking after me he'd rather I enjoyed school and university holidays and played sport and had a good time. He didn't believe that doing bar jobs from a young age would instil in me a better work ethic when I was older. I think he was right. And he was absolutely clear that the limit of his generosity was when I left higher education. From then on, I had to go and earn a living. That time had arrived.

In June 1998 I was able to drive again but was blagging my way through life in ways that even now seem pretty extreme. I sold my Alfa Romeo Cloverleaf and put the money into a deposit for a Lotus Elise I couldn't afford to buy. I traded several cars, which back in the days of cash deals and zero-overhead living made up the difference. The Elise was hot property back then, with people paying way over list price, so my plan was to flip the car and then get moving. Bag the cash and then order the other big movers: a Mercedes SLK, a Boxster and a BMW Z3. What a pathetic plan that looks like now, 25 years later.

Could I have made it work? I'm not sure, but I know that if one of my kids presented that as their grand plan into adult life, I'd take a deep breath, roll my eyes to the ceiling and be as supportive as possible. And prepare to write a cheque when it all went wrong.

And then Patrick Fuller called: 'I'll probably massively regret this, but I'm offering you a job as a road test assistant.' I still don't know what changed his mind.

THIRTEEN
FIRST DAY
AT WORK

There is perhaps nothing more middle class than a mother taking her son shopping in advance of him beginning his first job. Mine took me to London – always known as 'The Smoke' to us simple West Country folk – and bought me a very sharp blazer and a pair of slacks. She would probably have said something along the lines of: 'You need to look smart at work, dear – it gives the correct impression.' I probably wore that blazer twice over the next five years. I mean, why would you need a blazer to be a road test assistant?

That was a rhetorical question I didn't ask myself the first morning I took the train to Teddington to start my new job, wearing my new blazer and slacks. I must have looked like a tramp who had just robbed a Ralph Lauren store. But actually I was as brown as I'd ever been because the last month had been spent down in the south of France with my pal Rowan in my Lotus Elise.

I can't write a book about my life with cars and not mention R181 JHW. It was my first sports car, and any motor tragic naturally prioritises that above any other 'first' that might appear on the lists of normal men. The Elise was the most stupid thing I had ever bought – I'd flogged a few cars and scrambled some cash together. Much of this was based on the usual zero-overhead lifestyle that young people assume means they can afford anything because someone else is paying for their lives – in this case, I lived rent-free at my girlfriend's house.

One day I popped down to the Lotus garage in Bristol – I'm pretty sure what this constituted was a small corner of a Mazda franchise where an Elise and an Esprit lurked. The Elise was already the most talked-about British sports car in a generation, and I'd read the *Autocar* road test so many times I could quote the performance figures and most of the words too. This was the summer of 1997, the beginning of the specu-lation game in the UK and, as I've already mentioned, I tried to put a deposit on anything that I thought might get me into an 'overs' situation: SLK, Z3, Boxster and Lotus Elise. Now, attempting to blag your way into a Boxster was a little more tricky than an Elise because the local Porsche dealership could smell chancers like me a mile off, so I focussed on Norfolk's little lightweight gem first. The initial deposit was nothing – it might even have been as little as £500 – after which, very handily, there was no interim payment nonsense that always flushed out the true blagger, as most of us were trying to pre-sell the car, drive it off the forecourt to avoid suspicion and then hand it to the new owner asap. In the process, hopefully, trousering a decent profit.

The Elise arrived in the late spring of 1998. It was metallic blue and I loved it more than any car I had ever seen, let alone had access to on a daily basis. This was a machine that cost a little over £24,000 and yet turned as many heads as a new Ferrari F355. That probably won't be repeated again in the world of the motor car. I was 24 years old, totally fraudulent in my beautiful blue Lotus and, best of all, Patrick Fuller had just offered me a job beginning in the second week of September. Once I'd put fuel in the Lotus I didn't have a pot to piss in, but no one else knew that so I just swanned about Bristol for a while playing as much golf and cricket as possible. Most people who love cars cannot abide either of those sports, but I've always loved watching and playing both.

I find it very hard to deliver life lessons without cringing or wanting to laugh at the absurdity of an idiot like me imparting advice, but there are few things more enjoyable than having a plan that allows you to enjoy the days without a care because you have a concrete situation looming in the near future. You sleep the sleep of someone with no worries. You laugh more; people like you more. That was the summer of 1998.

It was during this idyllic period that the first thing went wrong with the Lotus Elise. Specifically, it suffered an acute bodywork malfunction at the hands of a Volvo 440.

I haven't mentioned many of my school pals by name because they probably wouldn't appreciate the attention, but one of them that would is a man called Tom Windows. Tommy, or Slug as he is known, is one of those personalities that loomed so large throughout my early years that, now I'm on telly, it feels quite odd that he didn't end up on the telly too. He is a natural in a way I never could be. He is a very large, very funny man. You need to know those things to appreciate his involvement in the first time it went wrong in the blue Lotus Elise.

Tommy had, and still has, zero interest in fast cars, but for some reason he came for a ride in the Elise. The little Lotus has easily the smallest cabin of anything I've owned shy of a Caterham and I can vaguely recall much of him being on top of me as we left Clifton Village, comfortably the poshest part of Bristol. We then headed towards somewhere called Ladies Mile which, back then, was a straight road whose length you can guess and which was part of a loop around the largest green area of Bristol: the Downs. This was the only place to give it some tap within the city. Amazingly, it was a national speed limit road back then – it's a 20mph zone now. Looking back, I can't believe it was legal to travel so fast there.

However, it was. And I was keen to demonstrate to Tommy Windows just how handy I was in this dramatic new sports car that he had zero interest in. We crossed over the historic Bridge Valley Road and on to the long, uphill right-hander. The road was damp. I gave it a prod of throttle to lightly provoke the back axle into a nice hip-shimmy – just like I had been doing for months with complete success. Only this time the little blue car behaved differently.

These were the days before traction control and all that jazz on sports cars. In fact, back then it was a badge of honour to have no safety systems at all – to the point that I'm not sure if the Elise even had a brake servo. You were on your own. And this also meant that you could quite easily convince yourself that you had complete control of a car under any circumstances because you'd managed to hang on to a couple of teeny-weeny drifty moments before. Come on, you know you've been there too – you antagonise the thing a little bit and then in your own head you're the absolute master of the machine!

Except that one time when you're not. When you're so limited and lacking in skill and experience that you don't for one minute realise that the change in road conditions will make the car do something quite different from anything you've experienced before. So I mashed the accelerator and waited for the rear Pirellis to step the familiar few feet wide, which they did. And then they kept sliding.

The first time you feel a slide completely get away from you I can guarantee that however much you might think you can recall what happened, you can't. The human brain in a state of panic is a chemical mess that will construct any fantasy to make the fallout less painful. I'm now somehow an expert on sliding cars and car control, but back then I didn't know shit. What I did know was that the blue Elise was already up a grass bank before big Tommy could utter his first piece of quality invective, and back down on the road before I had probably applied anything like a useful amount of corrective lock. The bank stopped us spinning, but it spat us back onto the wrong side of the road, where a Volvo 440 happened to be travelling in the opposite direction. Lotus connected with Volvo, and the result was as about as different as I could ever have expected.

As big Tommy attempted to extract himself from the Lotus, I jumped out to make sure the lady driving the Volvo was okay. Normally I'd use the word 'woman', but this person was of an age and demeanour that means she was most definitely a lady. She was physically fine and, both thankfully and unhelpfully, born of that stoical old-school stock that meant she very quickly got onto the front foot and started asking awkward questions.

What the hell did I think was doing? No answer to that one. Would I be calling the police? Not if I could help it. Was that my car? I could answer that one – yes, it was. Her gimlet-eyed stare suggested she didn't believe that last bit for one second.

This was the era before mobile phones were commonplace and it does demonstrate that they can be a force for good in these situations because they're an excellent conversation killer – people can recede and phone people, and generally hide from talking to one another. How I wish I could have hidden from her.

But we needed to get this lady going again asap and not rely on a recovery service – or worse, plod – and an initial inspection revealed a decent chance of doing just that. But the damage to the Volvo was remarkable. The entire length of the nearside was trashed – front wing, both doors and the rear quarter – whereas the Elise just had a cracked front clam. The tricky part was the punctured right-rear.

By now our lady was calm and, I felt, becoming mildly seduced by my charms. I sat her on the bank as I told her that myself and my friend (Tommy had squeezed himself out of the Lotus with an unhelpful volley of 'fuck's and 'my-fucking-back's, and was now stood by my side like an enormous ham) were here to assist her. We must have looked like a semi-Persian remake of *Dumb and Dumber.*

We set to work on the knackered wheel. The wheel brace happened to be on the back seat, so I cracked the nuts and asked my able assistant to open the boot and locate the jack. He did this, but there was enough clanking of belongings and God knows what to prick the attention of the good lady, whose response to me was once again slipping from the positive to the downright suspicious. I signalled that I was getting on with the job with a jolly wave and her forehead momentarily de-furrowed.

Tommy was utterly sodding useless at this point and, once he became bored with standing next to me and taking the piss, he moved his attention to the grass bank where he collected bits of the Lotus's blue bodywork and bought them back to me like a Labrador presenting unwanted doggy-treasures. This happened a couple of times, and I noticed a further negative change in the lady. She clearly thought we were blagging, so I suggested to Tommy that he head back to the boot of her car and make himself look busy in some way. For once, he complied.

But she still came over and rebooted the awkward questions. And then she decided to take control: 'I'm calling the police. You can't replace the wheel properly and I'm not happy ...'

She trailed off because both of us were now aware of a new noise coming from the boot of her car. There was rustling and some lighter metallic knocks. She immediately walked to the back of the car and, in a voice of the most perfect matronly exasperation, said: 'And what on earth do you think you're doing?'

I could see exactly what he was doing because I'd scuttled along behind her. He was eating a Scotch egg from her shopping. There's something very British about seeing a well-spoken woman of a certain age admonish a youth who could crush her with one hand. In fairness, Tommy was sniggering when he shrugged and said, 'Sorry, I was hungry.'

Matters moved quickly to a head. I begged her to let me finish changing the wheel while she guarded her weekly shop from Tommy's tummy. Ten minutes later, we were on our way.

The Elise took ages to fix because some crash structure was unavailable to buy. I drove it around damaged in the meantime, which was a mistake because the mickey-taking was merciless, and there's something quite disturbing about something as simple and beautiful as an S1 Elise with a punched face. The most obvious downside to being the 'car guy' of any group is the catastrophic judgement when you get it wrong in a car. Mostly it's well deserved, as it was in this case.

And then it was off to France. In a Lotus Elise with my friend Rowan. If you go to a posh school you end up with friends called Rowan.

I'd driven to France a few times before, but the sense of adventure wasn't in any way diminished – 25 years later it still isn't. Perhaps the one binding love throughout the diverse, weird and often conflicting world of cars is that everyone loves the process of a road trip. The preparation, the planning, the getting up hours before your body is accustomed to and luxuriating in the quiet roads and the emerging light and the people still dealing with the night before. I suppose we left Bristol at 4am and dashed to Folkestone. I can't actually remember, but I can guarantee that at that moment there was no place I'd have rather been.

This was just before the speed resistance ruined driving through France with radar traps and disturbingly tight trousers, so we pinned it, roof off, and went as fast the car would go. It would cruise at around 130mph, but the tiny little Stack fuel gauge's numbers would drop very quickly at that speed. (Nerd observation: has there ever been a cleaner, more perfect set of clocks than those found in an original Elise?)

Halfway through France the sun became more intense, and Rowan decided to buy a tin of cream for his ample forehead. Not sun cream, just Nivea moisturiser. Seven hours of sunshine later we arrived at our destination – a mostly derelict medieval priory his parents had bought – and he resembled a well-prepared pork belly.

For the next month we woke up, drove along fantastic winding French D-roads to the same beach and hurtled along a great stretch of autoroute to get home again. The Elise was a rock-star car: even in Norfolk where they built them it was a rare sight, but on the French Riviera it snapped necks. No one is immune to the appeal of people looking at them in a pretty motor car. I had never before been a peacock, and believe I am not one now, but in France in 1998 I flashed every feather I had.

During this time of unadulterated K-series-powered bliss, in the middle of thinking I was driving the only Lotus in that part of the world, I can remember seeing a silver Esprit on UK plates. An odd sighting and a little annoying once the euphoria of the reaction subsided into 'I thought I was in a class of one'.

Now, allow me to interrupt 1998 and fast forward a few years to when I was working at *Autocar*. I was telling someone from Lotus about that dreamy trip in my own Elise, and for whatever reason I mentioned seeing that Esprit. His face dropped: 'Are you sure it was silver?'

He then told me one of the greatest car press office/journalist stories I've ever heard. That silver Esprit was probably the most famous Lotus road car outside of the James Bond franchise. In early August 1998, a chap called Jonathan Kern called the Lotus press office and asked if he could book an Esprit to feature in *Now Magazine*. Lotus undertook the usual rigorous tests to corroborate who he was (phone book at best) and then delivered the car. Kern drove it to the Belgian Grand Prix, then telephoned Lotus to say it had been stolen. Then he headed towards the Mediterranean.

Turns out Kern was a trickster who had a history of blagging cars and taking them on extended (for that read many months long) test drives. And for the late summer of 1998 he fancied himself something Lotus-shaped. He ran up massive bills all over southern France and Italy posing as Jonathan Palmer.

Many of you will know of a racing driver called Jonathan Palmer. He won a curious thing called the Jim Clark Trophy, for non-turbo cars in a mostly turbo Formula 1 grid, in 1987. He's also a fully qualified medical doctor, an extremely sharp businessman who owns many of the UK racing circuits, and, the important bit, someone I would not like to tangle with. The idea of his PA fielding a call from an irate Italian prostitute chasing payment for services rendered – which did actually happen – does make me chuckle louder than I should.

Kern was eventually arrested, and the car was returned to Lotus. He was interviewed while serving his prison sentence for this and a few other shady episodes, and his response to taking the Esprit was the most perfectly brass-necked piece of British logic: 'I think Lotus have done well out of this. I've given them lots of publicity. I think they should pay me.'

If only I'd known how easy it was to swipe a free Lotus press car I wouldn't have gone to the considerable effort of buying one of the bloody things.

The second time the Lotus Elise went wrong? I think it was the clutch, and from memory it left me stranded in a very awkward place near Grasse. And I'm not going to talk about any of the others because that was the most perfect motor car for me and I don't want to traduce its memory.

People often look back at their lives and talk about boyfriends or girlfriends who were perfect for that time in their lives. That Elise filled that role – it was the first rear-wheel drive car I'd ever driven. It taught me to respect stuff that wasn't easy and front-driven. It instilled in me an affection for Lotus that will always exist, and it introduced me to the joys of driving with no roof.

And I still haven't told you about that first day at *Autocar*. Apologies.

FOURTEEN
FIRST DAY AT WORK (AGAIN)

The blazer was ditched before I walked into the office. Of course it was. I was given a seat at a desk with two drawers and a computer that had a black-and-white screen. I was also given a little pot of business cards that read 'Chris Harris, Road Test Assistant'. It could have said 'Secretary General of the UN' and I wouldn't have been more proud. A few people in the office were welcoming, a few weren't, but I just couldn't believe how lucky I was.

The first thing I ever did as a motoring journalist was drive a BMW E39 528i automatic to the Chobham test track down on the M3 where it needed photographing. Presumably I just walked around in a daze for a while and then drove back to the office. I went home, or rather to the sofa I was sleeping on, in a brand-new Jaguar XJR. This was all so mind-scramblingly cool that I didn't really know how to react.

The simple concept of having a job was probably, and for a series of rather embarrassing reasons, more of an epiphany for me than most. I don't need to repeat how unseriously I'd taken life, or how little academic work I'd ever done. The only nagging question I have now, in hindsight, is whether my father had a rare foresight that meant he was sure that at some point I'd wake up and become a functioning member of society. Or if he was impish enough to find mirth in propelling something as unfinished as me into an unsuspecting world.

What occurred without me realising it was I worked hard. It's difficult to define a verb for that sentence because I didn't really see it as work – this activity quickly became the focus of my entire life and I discovered a work ethic that no one who had known me until that point would ever have believed possible. I would do anything at *Autocar*, just so long as it meant spending time at *Autocar*.

The first corollary of this was that I started to sleep like I never had before, because apart from a few nights on the piss and the odd hockey game, my body had never really been tired before. I'd get back from work at seven or eight in the evening and want to go straight to bed. Then I'd be up at seven the next day and raring to go.

I needed to push hard because I had an arch nemesis at *Autocar* in the form of a chap called Alistair Weaver. He was given a job at the same time as me, with the same job title, but there were a couple of small differences. He had just graduated from Oxford University with something impressive and I had just been asked not to come back to Oxford Brookes having failed to gain third-class honours. He was also, as far as I could tell, immensely confident in his ability to write and, the really tricky bit, he'd started a few weeks before me. I was on the back foot from the start.

Competitive spirit is something we don't necessarily attempt to understand or unpack until much later in life. In my case it's taken being a parent myself and managing how my kids deal with their competitive urges to understand what those feelings have done to me over time. I am hopelessly competitive in just about everything I do. I want to win – not at all costs – but I seem to identify targets and rivals and use those to have something to spur me on. And there is always a strategy that emerges, a way of getting ahead of the opposition. And that's how I viewed Alistair Weaver. He wasn't the most important, he just happened to be the first I encountered in the workplace. There have been many others. In fact, if I were to peer into the mirror for too long I'd have to admit that I view everyone as the opposition apart from a few close friends. Does that make me a nutjob? Perhaps.

This was confusing, though. It was a dream job, and my boss was Steve Sutcliffe so I was learning from the best and spending a large percentage of my time laughing and having fun. But it was quite clear that 12 months on from myself and Alistair starting, there would only be one job at *Autocar*. The fight was on.

To win a fight you have to identify what the strengths of your opponent are, and what your own are. Before even attempting to formulate a plan you need to ask one question: 'Can I win this?' If the answer is yes, as I believed it was at the time, then crack on.

A head-to-head may seem brutal, but you learn so much about yourself from those skirmishes. If you'd told me that my main skill was simply being able to work harder than those around me, I just wouldn't have believed you. But it turns out I had a good engine and could put in more hours than my colleagues, so I looked busy. Bosses love it when people look busy.

And I could drive a bit. Not in the way many of the other members of staff could, and miles away from the likes of Steve, but whenever he told me to do something, or let me loose to try sliding or whatever it was, even though the skills didn't land immediately, nothing ever presented itself as being completely foreign or unachievable.

The biggest problem was learning to write, something I had never taken for granted, but had quietly hoped wouldn't be too tricky. Finding a voice would take some time, and it wouldn't happen in that first year.

So given what a shambles working life could have been, it was actually all going to plan. I thought I was establishing myself as the chosen one for the role going forwards when one Saturday a family friend phoned me and said, 'I'm sorry to have to tell you this, Chris, but your father passed away earlier this morning.'

And it all went to shit for a bit. I have never suffered FOMO more than those few months. I spent most of my time back in Bristol trying to look after my mother, and all the while I was worrying that Weaver was going to win! Mum was a pretty ferocious competitor, and had her head been in a better place I'd like to think she'd have understood.

And I did win. Alistair went off to the sister magazine *What Car?* and life was a bit smoother because I didn't wake up every morning with the need to do battle and beat someone. People who like competition suffer from one very obvious flaw – they cannot identify the moment beyond which the competitive spice becomes a contaminant, and rather than dragging better performance from themselves it begins to have a detrimental effect on life. That was definitely happening to me.

That first year had been a blur of new car experiences. The joy of *Autocar* for someone new and keen to get going as fast as possible was it being a weekly magazine. The turnover of machinery and stories was so high I could create a new experience pretty much daily. And my bosses, Steve and Patrick, supported that by ensuring I was exposed to as many new cars and people as possible. The latter was a slight risk because I was and still am quite capable of getting it very wrong with other human beings.

Within six months of starting that first job I'd driven an example of most models of new car being sold in the UK. That's the beginning of your car-testing database and it allows you to just build and build with every further interaction. If that reads like a very sad thing to read from a bloke who presents *Top Gear*, I need to admit that remains my priority today. I love motor cars and very little interests me as much as getting behind the wheel and working out if they're any good or not. It's certainly more interesting than filming a television show.

I had also been to my first few car launches. And they were completely ridiculous. Only recently have carmakers stopped earmarking a decent chunk of a car's development budget to host a swanky event that allows journalists the opportunity to go and eat food and drink too much free wine. And maybe at some point drive the car.

Honestly, the first few car launches I attended were a total shock to the system, and if I'd been less obsessed with cars and driving anything with four wheels, they probably would have made me want to find a different job. I think the first was for something called a Mitsubishi Space Star in somewhere completely ordinary like Brussels. But the second was for the facelift first-generation Audi A8, and it was in Monaco – or a slither of France so close to Monaco it might as well have been the principality.

The trip went like this. We were flown, at the front of the plane, to Nice Airport, then shuttled to a swanky hotel on a hill that I think had a lift that went down a cliff face. Even as a spoilt child, it was comfortably the swankiest hotel I'd ever stayed in. I was taken to my room, where sitting on my bed was some kind of gift in a bag. I'm not sure what it was, but long before there was even a chance of driving this luxury saloon that would, at best, be sold by the handful in the UK, the whole thing felt very smelly. I knew that carmakers held these events and the majority of them were overseas from the UK, but the extent to which they would smother journalists with situations that might somehow influence their review was bordering on comedic.

As were the established journalists. A few of them I knew from seeing their bylines in the bigger magazines and news-papers, and on the whole those ones did seem to view the absurd trappings being afforded them as a kind of necessary pretence to get to the car in question. But the others? What a shitshow.

A bigger swamp of talentless liggers you couldn't hope to meet. Most of them were there to sup on the free Audi booze and swan about like they deserved to live that lifestyle. Audi didn't seem to give a monkey's because all it really wanted was positive reviews, and if these lemmings were willing to be bought then that was hardly the fault of the carmaker.

Every launch had its dinner, during which, when you had some experience, you tried to avoid the worst people in the room. But as a rookie I had no idea who most of these people were, so I ended up sitting next to a chap from *What Car?* who (I later discovered) everyone thought was a disaster. Initially he was bearable, but after the meal, as people had a drink in some bar overlooking Monaco, and as his hands wandered around the waistline of some poor woman from Audi, he beckoned me over and said, 'Come and have a drink, you might learn something.'

Most people of my age look back on our early careers through the prism of 2023 value systems and shudder. Whatever aspects of today's way of interacting with others I may find ridiculous, and there are many, it in no way explains or justifies some of the hideousness we all witnessed back in the day.

During that first year I was driving some new Toyota in Ireland and there was, as usual, a lunch stop on the route. Even in 1998 they were offering out booze, and the majority of the old-timers accepted – most of them were a complete danger when driving sober. But when one of these creatures aggressively gestured for the Indian waiter to come and refill his glass, he called him 'Sinbad'. I didn't much like anything about that so went and told someone from Toyota that a man who was about to drive a car having drunk too much booze to legally do so had just racially abused a member of staff. The man from Toyota sort of grimaced and suggested I should probably just leave lunch and get going so I didn't have to listen to the chap anymore.

That sounds outrageous now, but it probably felt like a sensible way of dealing with the situation back then. Whichever way I look at it, the UK motoring journalist community in 1998 was mostly a cesspit. It was almost entirely male, white and so saturated with all of the grim prejudices you'd expect from a group of such people that I do feel a sense of guilt that I allowed myself to swim among them. It probably peaked when I was told that, in my absence, the boss of comms for BMW GB said about me: 'His sort don't know how to treat women anyway.'

There were several ways to avoid this side of the car industry, though. The first was to climb the greasy pole of seniority and bag more important work for *Autocar* magazine that would take me away from the launch circuit. Bigger features and group tests – the stuff I'd always wanted to be doing. The other was to try and propagate a few 'friendships' that would mean the chance of a friendly face or two if I did have to go to those events.

This was the era of grey-import Japanese hotrods, and they were box office for car magazines. If you popped a Scooby or an Evo on the cover of the magazine, sales went up 10 per cent and everyone was happy. But none of the really juicy stuff appeared officially in the UK, so we had to build relationships with the specialist dealers who would fly the cars in from Japan the moment they could buy them. I spent much of my time trying to blag my way into this stuff. They were fantastic cars to drive. The world was rally-mad back then – McRae was a global superstar, Grönholm was dominant and the Subaru vs Mitsubishi rivalry was as emotive as anything the car world had seen before. A good Mitsubishi Evo VI GSR would still take care of most things down a UK B-road.

If the discovery that I could work harder and longer hours than most remained really quite surprising, my utter obsession with being able to drive well probably wasn't. I wanted to be able to drive like my boss, Steve, and he was generous enough to help me at every opportunity. And as anyone who has tried to learn to slide a car will tell you, there can be no progress without pain.

After the usual glib 'What's your favourite car of all time?' question, the most common thing I'm asked about is how I learnt to drive. Actually, the second most common thing I'm asked is whether Paddy McGuinness is actually funny in real life, which of course he isn't, so the driving one is more pertinent.

I learnt to drive by being very interested in driving. And that meant I was always watching how people drove. I spent hours watching how people operated the controls: the way they'd excite a vehicle into a slide, how they'd control it, the way they'd balance throttle and brake and feel their way in to all of this. None of that would have been possible if I didn't have the chance to sit next to people of very high skill, and luckily I did.

And this perceived obsession with sliding motor cars that I'm regularly accused of wasn't just about being able to do cool stuff. That was a large part of it, but there was a very practical consideration too. This was the era of still photography, and that meant the tools available to show people images that supported the words were limited. If you wrote about how the latest BMW M3 was a doozy to slide and then the photographs showed that very car nose-ploughing into the outside of a corner, then the package didn't work.

I just wanted to be able to do this in front of a photographer to demonstrate how I had written about the car. That meant pleading for time at the end of every photoshoot to practise how to do this in every conceivable type and configuration of car. It took some time, but before long it was becoming easier. The most important thing was to not overreach yourself; not to persuade yourself that you had control of something you really didn't. Doing that was the best way to lose your job.

These, I now realise, were the halcyon days of my working life. I now make way more money and have what most people would understandably consider to be the best job in the world. But I'm a grown-up now and have responsibilities, and the public highway isn't somewhere you can behave like we used to. My best job was that first job: road test assistant at *Autocar*. I loved learning, I loved working hard and I started to get along well with many of the people I worked with. The only slight problem was that I earned so little money that any normal human being would have tempered the joy of the workplace with the knowledge that it was unlikely they'd ever be able to afford to live. But who gives a crap about affording a bigger flat or having a holiday if you get to go to the launch of the new E39 M5, or fly to Germany to drive the first Porsche GT3 back to the UK? Not me.

FIFTEEN
MY FIRST
PORSCHE

In April 1989 *Fast Lane* ran a test of the most exciting fast cars available in the UK. They drove them around Donington Park and the story appeared on the cover. None of this was especially noteworthy – other mags had tested all of these cars before.

The difference this time was that they had recorded each of the cars being spanked around the circuit by writer and racing driver Mark Hales. A cassette of these purely audio recordings was then stuck to the front of the magazine cover. People of my age will confirm how we were all total suckers for any free tat on the cover of a mag. But this was different. It wasn't a keyring or a cleaning cloth – it was a new type of content.

The three cars I remember Mark driving were a Ferrari F40, a Ford Sierra Sapphire Cosworth, and a Porsche 911

Club Sport. That cassette was one of my prized possessions for many years. I would listen to it on my Walkman when all the normal children listened to Michael Jackson, which must have made me look like the weirdo at the time but ended quite well for me.

If someone were to ask me to define the point at which a hobby becomes an obsession, admitting listening to a man drive some cars around a track is a good place to start. The cars featured on the *Fast Lane* track test in 1989 were probably my heroes.

Fast forward ten years and Porsche Swindon has a 1988 911 Club Sport for sale. I had just managed to secure quite a significant pay rise and sell a couple of cars as a side hustle and went along to the garage to see it. This was the weekend I'd driven something called a 911 GT3 back to the UK from Germany to give it the full *Autocar* road-test treatment. This was perhaps my first exposure to the intoxicating feeling of enjoying something money couldn't buy, and this was, I believe, the incentive for many of us hacks back then.

I arrived to look at an old, mostly forgotten 911, driving the latest performance car from Porsche – truly dog-with-two-dicks territory. The 17-year-old me just wouldn't believe that this had come to pass. And to put it in context, sitting here thinking about how I felt that day surfaces much more powerful memories than anything to do with fame or television. You could have been the best Porsche customer in the world and there wasn't a GT3 for you to borrow in July 1999, let alone buy. But the press cars did exist, and *Autocar*'s calling card was strong enough to put us on the list. This one even had the obligatory set of S-GO German plates on it. The irony is that I would become so closely associated with the Porsche GT3 over the next two decades that people genuinely thought I worked for the company.

The man at Porsche was called Matthew Beard and we must have got on well because I played golf with him last week. The car had done 28k miles and was perfect. It was identical to the one featured on the *Fast Lane* tape. Then I had a poke around the service history and found that it had been a press car for Porsche GB and registered with the number plate OPR 911. It was the actual car from the *Fast Lane* tape recording. Non-car-saddos will never understand the importance us nerds place on such seemingly meaningless connections, but they mean everything.

I sold the Elise and raised the extra few thousand pounds needed by taking out a couple of credit cards, and away we went. I had never driven a 911 this old, but what could possibly be wrong with a limited edition, lightweight Porsche? Initially, quite a lot, it turns out. The pedal box was a disaster – hinged from the floor and seemingly unkeen to help the driver action any input smoothly. To be able to kick those pedals I had to sit way too close to the wheel, which was the strange four-spoke thing taken from a 928. The car fitted me like a school uniform on the first day of a new school year. Itchy. I was tempted to turn round and ask for the Lotus back.

I kangaroo'd my way out of Swindon in a whale-tailed white 1980s Porsche complete with red writing down the sides

– looking every inch like a plonker with no idea how to drive it. An hour later I was completely in love with that little white car. The Porsche 911 has always been a weirdo that requires a muscle memory reset. Even if it's only been a few days since you last drove one, the seat will feel awkward and you'll wish the steering would adjust in some other way, and the strange pedals might be less annoying if they were actually directly underneath the wheel. And yet within a few miles – bingo! – your body will adapt and you're back in that favourite pair of slippers.

This was my first Porsche. The posters on my bedroom and boarding school study walls had been Porsches. One of the few areas where the Venn diagram of life overlaps between nerds and ordinary people is the aspirational purchase of a motor car. The difference between the two groups is that for one of them this represents just a single part of an accumulation of life goals. For the other it is all-consuming. Nothing else matters.

Even when I wasn't driving that Porsche, I would just sit in it like a zombie. I would walk past it and assume it was someone else's. I'm not a polisher – I wouldn't remove parts of the car and clean them, but, subliminally, driving that car was my default preferred activity. People like me engineer situations that might result in them needing to pop out for a drive.

This wasn't a car I could leave on the street in London, so I asked my father if I could stash it in his double garage. Like any dad, his garage was his, and anything that didn't belong to him in there was under suspicion of being contraband. I arrived in my white Porsche with red writing down the side, six months after I'd had to ask him to help me pay my rent. Yes, life moves fast and circumstances can change, but this was taking the piss. He completely ignored the car, told me to see if it would fit next to his Audi and then walked inside.

Who do we want to acknowledge our successes? I must have wanted my father to look at me and think 'boy done good', but that wasn't going to happen because I was 24 and hadn't achieved anything at all.

I took the Porsche to the Nürburgring six times. I would travel on my own and sometimes meet other people there. In my first month at *Autocar* I'd watched a VHS video of a car called the RUF Yellowbird – a crazy modified Porsche 911 Turbo – being driven around this incredible circuit, sliding at angles that still seem impossible 40 years after it was filmed.

For those of you who don't know what the Nürburgring is, it's the longest, most challenging, most dangerous racetrack in the world. It's four times longer than Silverstone and wriggles around some very hilly north-German countryside. But most of you know that, or you wouldn't have picked up this book.

I bonded with my first Porsche on trips to the Nürburgring. I learnt the circuit slowly and methodically – skills I'd never deployed before that time. I didn't have any tuition from any pros, but I would ask the people I saw going quickly if I could sit next to them and just watch their lines and the way they controlled the car – the places they took a few risks and the places they didn't. The danger zone at the Nürburgring is when you think you know it, probably after 20 laps, and then you suddenly realise that you don't. There aren't many small accidents there, and a rather rare late-eighties Porsche is perhaps the most stupid machine to choose for those purposes.

On one of these trips, I was heading to the Channel Tunnel very early, around 5am, and was making good time when I felt the urge to let the Porsche run a bit. This is an occasional urge every car person is subjected to, and in 2023 it has become a risky pastime. The debate over speed and safety has run for years and ever-more uninformed voices now claim that speed is more dangerous than a heroin-laced death-cap mushroom. But those of us with half a brain know this is utter bollocks. The inappropriate deployment of speed is the dangerous bit. Speed itself is a brilliant thing and separates us from the beasts. You might now have an inkling where this story is headed.

The sun is rising, the white Porsche is heading towards the fatherland at a speed far more in keeping with its original design intentions than the measly 70mph dictated by His Majesty's Government. The motorway is completely empty and I can see for at least two miles ahead. The speed rises steadily in an old Porsche 911 – at around 100mph the engine is still the dominant noise in the cabin, and the smooth drone of the fan and those six cylinders overcomes the wind noise generated from the protruding rubber windscreen surrounds and guttering. As the numbers rise, the power struggle between engine and wind noise moves in favour of the latter. The engine is reduced to a whisper – a beautiful, expensive-sounding whisper – as the air is deflected away from awkward shapes with increased energy and begins to shout louder.

I was probably enjoying these changes when I spotted a car parked on the hard shoulder. Even with a decent closing speed the committed car-saddo can tell what make and model of car they're dealing with and whether it might be something used by the constabulary. In that instant, my brain told me it was a Peugeot 405 and therefore nothing police related. A few tenths of a second later when I saw the man peering over the open front door and pointing something the shape of a radar gun at the white Porsche, things felt a little different. That bolt of fear we all experience in such situations shot down my spine and into my tailbone. I thought immediately about stopping, but that seemed ridiculous, so I merely reduced the speed back to a less extreme number and continued on my way, with my eyes scanning all three mirrors like my life depended on it.

Then you process the inner questions. The voice in your head. What did I actually see? Was it really a Peugeot? How long would that car take to accelerate to a speed where it might catch me? And, by association, how much time must elapse before I can safely say that this isn't going to happen and become a massive problem? A life-changing problem?

I was just beginning to allow my body to relax when the Peugeot appeared in the mirror. There's no doubt I could have just pinned the Porsche and disappeared into a different county, such was the speed advantage, but that didn't feel like the best decision, so I slowed a little and allowed it to come alongside. I looked at the driver who was gesturing with one hand quite aggressively. He then pulled in front and slowed down, indicating left. This didn't feel good.

He came to the passenger-side window. His emotional state was hard to decipher: perplexed, a little angry and somehow frustrated. He showed me his badge and asked me how fast I thought I'd been travelling. I said I didn't know, because we were all taught that at the very beginning. He then told me that he had recorded me at a speed which I will not write here because it will increase my already good chances of being cancelled. But I will admit that somewhere in the soup of emotions there was a hint of pride. That was a very good speed. As the policeman was then layering on some more details I can remember thinking that I really should be concentrating on what he was saying, but my blasted brain was gabbling away: 'That's a good speed, Chris, in fact, what's the claimed top speed for a 911 Club Sport? We might even have nudged beyond it.'

The policeman continued. But he didn't move into fines or court appearances or anything like that. He then said that his reason for being there was to calibrate a new speed gun. The equipment, he said, was not yet authorised to be used in the UK and wouldn't support a court prosecution. This is a long time ago now, but I'm pretty sure he took one look at the fear in my face and thought that was enough, that he'd done his job. There was a brief attempt at a lecture, but the speed was so high I now think the longer he engaged with me the more angry he feared he would become.

I made one good decision that day – not to run. That would have resulted in helicopters and newspapers and court appearances and the early end to an already average career.

There was something about that Peugeot that didn't look like plod. I don't know if it's an urban myth, but I was always taught that a single police officer can't nick you for a speeding offence, and seeing one bloke on his own must have registered. As worrying as the whole situation might have seemed – and it evolved in under a second – there was enough doubt to make me think that if I stopped the consequences might not be as catastrophic as feared.

I kept the car for nearly four years. It didn't require anything more than routine maintenance. In 2003 I was in the process of growing up – getting married and buying a house in the countryside – and the Porsche had to be sold. It went for £28,500. They are now worth over £200,000, but selling cars which then become very valuable is a theme for a future chapter. In this case that sum of money provided a grim symmetry with the house purchase, which had generated a stamp duty liability of exactly £28,500. I effectively gave Gordon Brown the car I've loved the most during my life.

That was the beginning of a total love affair with the Porsche 911. I have lost count of how many I've owned, but they are a constant in my life and they made every drive just a little bit better than if it was undertaken in a lesser vehicle. I have owned far more exotic and desirable versions, but that is the one I'd want back in my garage now. I could recall all the memories, even the naughty ones. And because it was there the day I last spoke to my father before he died – when I asked him for that garage space.

SIXTEEN
THE BEST
YEARS OF MY
WORKING LIFE

'You must have the best job in the world, buddy.'

This is the most common thing people say to you when you are lucky enough to present *Top Gear*. It's a fair assumption, and I can confirm that I am a very lucky bastard to have such a job. But working at *Autocar* as a staff member, and then for many years as a kind of permanent freelance writer, was better.

From 1998 to 2007 I wrote hundreds of thousands of words for that magazine. The automotive industry is now in such a state of crisis that I think we can identify that period as a golden era in the history of the motor car – and especially the fast car. The economy was stable, house prices were rising and most cars cost sensible money. And the audience for these fast cars was big. *Top Gear* had rebooted into a studio format, and I always felt that show was the unofficial marketing department for the wider car media industry. As more and more people tuned in to see Jeremy and his sidekicks do their thing, so they might be tempted to delve further into the geekier corners of the newsstand and pick up a copy of *evo* or *Autocar*.

And cars became good in that era. When I first started in the job it was still possible to find some genuinely awful new cars. Most of them were Korean – which shows how quickly that country has developed into a maker of world class EVs. Or they were American, and sometimes from the UK. But they were out there. By 2007 it was genuinely hard to find a bad new car – as in something that wouldn't complete a journey, would corrode and which drove with zero sophistication.

Of course, there were a few early on. The Kia Rio was so bad *Car Magazine* channelled Duran Duran's 1982 hit for a one-line review: 'Her name is Rio … and she's crap.'

There were some mechanically sound but very, very vanilla machines too. The Mazda 626 was so reliable it would never die, which was a shame because there's no way anyone would have wanted to buy one in 1999. Even so, Mazda duly delivered one to the *Autocar* office, and it garnered a very small, unfavourable review in the 'First Drives' section of the magazine. This would have simply been disappointing for Mazda if it didn't have a record of the mileage covered by the car during its time with us – 0.0 miles to be precise. I won't say who wrote the review.

Everything was new and fun, and I was surrounded by people I liked. Colin Goodwin was a brilliant features writer who sometimes gave the impression he was from this planet. That makes him sound like he's dead when he's anything but. He didn't like me at first, then six months into the job he announced that actually I was alright, and I don't think we stopped laughing for the next seven years. Goodwin's brand of car enthusiasm was wonderfully eclectic – he found joy in things many others overlooked, and he loved spannering.

Most of us just liked driving things and writing, but Col wanted to buy a Chevy El Camino in the US and then rebuild the engine himself. In Surrey. I stayed on his sofa for a while because I was lobbed out of a flat, and all off his clothes lived around his living area because the chest of drawers was full of engine components. He had allowed his passion for mechanical things to completely overwhelm his life, and he was proud to share that with people in the way he spoke and the way he wrote. He was once sitting in the office being asked why he hadn't bought a flat. 'What class can you race a flat in at Brands Hatch?' was his response. Puerile and childish: but exactly how I thought about cars. This was something powerful and new for me because for so many years I'd internalised my love for cars, being worried people would assume I was a wonk.

It also changed the way I wrote about cars. I'm not a writing talent like a Russell Bulgin, or a Setright, but I did find some kind of a voice early on. And it was Goodwin who helped me do that – he once said after reading something of mine that was hopelessly overcomplicated that I should just type the way I talked about cars. Amazing how one innocuous conversation sandwiched between whether Jochen Rindt had the best helmet design of the seventies and what it would cost to run a Formula 5000 car can completely change the way a person writes.

Colin has always been a good friend to me, and he was uniquely placed to understand what it was like for me getting the *Top Gear* job, and the pressures that came with it, because he also happens to be a very old pal of James May. Who is also a very kind man, but more of him later.

If Goodwin was a standard bearer for just enjoying the life of cars and going with the flow, my total inspiration at the time – and still today – is a man called Peter Robinson. Unless you read car magazines a couple of decades ago, you probably won't know who he is, but to me he will always be the greatest-ever motoring journalist. Clarkson is a better writer and broadcaster, but Robbo is the king journo.

From day one, working with Peter was like being enrolled in the most fun school you could ever imagine. Even a quarter of a century ago he was sporting a white beard, and tall people (he's 6ft 4in) always have a headmasterly air about them. A blunt Aussie who would only accept the very hardest-working individuals, he was for many years the best thing about *Autocar* for me – you can tell there were many other people I frankly adored working with, but Robbo was the boss.

Very few people know how much of the way contemporary media approaches cars can be traced back to a few Australians in the early 1970s. There would be no current

Top Gear if a handful of talented young writers hadn't felt the need to sample Marmite instead of Vegemite. Ian Fraser, Mel Nichols and Steve Cropley were the voices that defined *Car Magazine* in its pomp – the one I used to read in the back of classrooms. It was a reaction to the stale, empirical work of 'testing' cars. It was about stories and people and humour and subverting the conventional way of approaching the subject. Sound familiar? Jeremy, Richard and James did it brilliantly on telly, but these Aussies were at it decades earlier. It's undeniable that one influenced the other.

Robbo arrived a little later. He wasn't one of the *Car* crew, but he was still royalty. To finish his career, he and his wife Erica decided to move to Italy and sample the good life. He would be European Correspondent for *Autocar*, which meant he built an impressive address book and became the person who fought to get into the latest cars first. That was the epicentre of the game back then – getting the story first. If you could blag the access, drive it, photograph it and get it on the cover for next Wednesday, you were ahead of your rivals and you were winning. Robbo was critical in persuading mostly German and Italian car companies to let us have the best access.

To maximise the efficiency of his time with these new cars, the magazine would often get a rival model delivered for the photoshoot, so the initial story would be a single drive and the following week there would be a comparison with the main rival, or rivals. This is where the fun was to be had. Peter was based in northern Italy and many of the shoots would happen there. Others were in the Alps for the obvious scenery benefits, or they were smash-and-grab events within sight of the main VW/Audi/BMW/Mercedes/Porsche factories. The main thing was, someone needed to be there to drive the other cars or, the very best outcome, someone had to drive to those locations in the rival cars from the UK.

And that was the best part of the best days of my working life. Waking with the sparrows and hacking across Europe in random cars – sometimes in convoy, sometimes solo – to random destinations with nothing but a map. I loved cars, but I also loved the journey – and it always had to be disorganised. Not just because I am without doubt the least organised person on the planet, but because it has been proven time and time again that some element of chaos makes every caper more fun. Hotel rooms were never booked, ferries and trains were blagged and the destination was always found, eventually.

And the first person I would see was Robbo with his huge gold-and-silver smile, and the knowledge that the next few days would be saturated with real hard work and laughter. We did work really hard. And we cared about the process of testing cars to the most obsessive level – in a way that would be difficult to explain to normal civilians without looking like complete weirdos. Pound coins were thrust against panel gaps, bodies were wedged into footwells to identify the source of mechanical noises. Notebooks were filled, serious discussions were had about the damping behaviour of cars whose potential owners wouldn't have even understood, least of all cared about. But we just wanted to be rigorous. And with Peter, if you worked hard, you were allowed to play hard, just so long as you were present-and-correct the following morning. I was being paid to do this, but I'd have paid to be allowed to go on those adventures.

There is no place for the word 'fearless' in the world of motoring journalism. It is quite possibly the least worthy of all the journalisms, but Robbo was the toughest character in our world. He ran his team with a simple code: we were on the side of the magazine reader, the car buyer, not the car company CEO. So long as you could justify your position and it wasn't a cheap shot, car companies were there to be tangled with. This was borne out to absolute perfection in his relationship with Luca Montezemolo, then boss of Ferrari and unquestionably the finest automotive CEO of his generation. Peter was in many ways completely in awe of Luca, but that didn't stop him challenging him at every opportunity and always asking the questions no one else had the balls to ask. I have a picture of him in my mind on the Ferrari Geneva International Motor Show stand, the place perhaps even beyond the famous Maranello factory where a Ferrari CEO is untouchable; a rock star with every eye on him.

As Ferrari's best customers and the world's press shimmied out of Luca's way, in stormed Peter to challenge him on something he'd decided needed airing (probably the lack of seat height adjustment on the 360 Spider, or something similarly crucial) and a heated discussion ensued, during which the much taller Robbo was jabbing his index finger into Luca's chest. I'd wager no one else has ever done that to

Mr Montezemolo. Sometimes it spilt over and got nasty, and I'm sure Peter still takes some pride in telling people he's had a life ban from Ferrari – twice.

Often it was me and Steve Sutcliffe who would end up on these adventures. We would be giggling like children even before we arrived – mostly in anticipation of hearing Robbo's brilliant Italian-Antipodean vocabulary, which from memory consisted of *tangenziale* (ring road) and *insalata con rucola* (rocket salad).

I would do whatever it took to tease these morsels from Robbo, and then when he said them we'd melt with laughter. I love the Australian accent – it's the finest of them all. It can be tender and harsh, it never sounds lazy or slurred and it supports honest, direct, quality swearing like no other. Only in Oz can they suffuse swearing with genuine love – and Robbo was world-class even among his kin. As we laughed at several '*tangenziales*', he'd treat us to another flash of that metallic grin and say, perfectly gently, 'Ah, fuck off, you blokes.' It goes without saying that when the Ashes was on, the friendship cooled.

We skidded Lamborghinis and Paganis with Peter. We covered the launches of what would become some of the greatest cars ever built like the BMW E39 M5 and E46 M3. He was at the heart of all the adventures, and when we drank a little too much, or a hedge was lightly rearranged, he'd cover for us and then issue the expected bollocking before smiling and moving on. I was so, so lucky to work with him and share those memories.

Occasionally these adventures would get a little bit spicy, but what would be the story of the month nowadays was just something we'd barely mention back then. I think the time I came closest to deciding 'I probably need to avoid any lengthy European road trips for a while' was driving back from the former East Germany in an Aston DB9 after the launch of some Porsche 997 variant.

The Aston decided it didn't want to hurry back to Blighty and slumped into limp-home mode, which left me barely able to keep ahead of the German trucker community. Ten hours later I arrived at the Channel Tunnel with a new level of hatred for a motor car and just wanted to get on the train. Ahead of me were what looked like four Chinese business-men in a rented VW Passat. They were struggling to move the car close enough to hand over their passports, the immigration officer was losing patience and the whole shambles looked like a Benny Hill sketch that didn't make the cut. The few people who know me well will confirm that I am shame-fully short on patience and temper. But I sat there watching this shambles and didn't succumb. This was 2004, and the semi-automatic-toting gendarmes no doubt influenced my decision not to get out and ask what the arse was going on.

The trouble started when the Passat's occupants started moving around and the car rolled slightly backwards. I gave a light toot of the horn to let them know they were moving, which of course cajoled Les Rambos into life. Just at the moment they decided to pay greater attention to the only two cars attempting to board a midnight train, the Passat trundled back much further, and faster. Straight into the front of the Aston.

The emotional response to this was initially confusing. I was glad the bastard Aston, which had made me an object of pure hatred for the truckers of northern Germany, had taken a biff on the nose. But I was also a little angry because these people didn't even get out to apologise, they just drove forwards again. I decided to go and have a word with them, but before I could cover the ten yards between the respective drivers' doors, a man with a large gun was standing in my way. He spoke very good English, but because I was now a little angry I still wanted to have a chat with the Passat driver, despite the large gun.

This didn't go down too well with the man holding the weapon. Many hours later, when they released me, they did acknowledge that the Aston was a pretty car. And told me the next train would be in four hours' time.

The Channel Tunnel became a focal point for all those later adventures – the symbolic start and finish location for trips that wouldn't be possible now. One obsession was trying to keep up with the Eurostar late at night between Arras and Paris on the A1 autoroute. I used to wait until night-time and then see if I could peg the train – which would cruise at 186mph – because I had this romantic idea that if just one passenger looked out of the window and, instead of seeing swarms of cars being overtaken by the train, spotted a lone shape tracking them at exactly their speed, they might point and say, 'He's going well.' I did manage it, several times. But I don't think any of the passengers ever saw.

The only other times the authorities took a dim view of us arriving at the train were both superbly childish. When a colleague found someone had stashed adult literature in the glovebox of the test car he was driving to embarrass him at the security check, he was wise to this and disposed of it out of the window a few miles before he arrived. Sadly for him the car he was driving had a significant rear wing and a few pages had wrapped themselves around the leading edge. His chat with customs was awkward.

And I did become a little too comfortable drifting the entire off-ramp on the UK side. They had a quiet chat with me and I stopped doing it. It's now in very poor condition, and a bit of me thinks it's a smart way of stopping idiots doing such things.

There was only one rule in among all of this: we only told people we trusted what we got up to. There were no videos, no pictures, no social media. I think it was an *omertà* built on the fear of the fun being taken away from us, which we all knew it would at some point. But for many years, the man who owned Haymarket Publishing paid for me to rag fast cars around Europe. He's called Michael Heseltine.

It came to an end because of the internet. Free content placed unsustainable burdens on the newsstand and suddenly writers had to produce a story for the magazine and one for the website and get some video footage. And suddenly the beautifully simple concept of the three-day, three-car photoshoot was in trouble because the advertising revenues were shrinking.

CHAPTER SIXTEEN

There were other structural issues, one of which really piqued my interest. For the majority of my working life until that point, the big car magazine brands had ruled the business. There were a handful of European magazines, the same number of US mags and Jeremy Clarkson, who was probably already bigger than all of the others put together.

Those brands owned the relationships with the carmakers. And they protected them. It was to them that the invitations to drive new products were sent, and in a world where first meant winning, they were always in charge. But towards the end of 2006 I noticed some changes. Those carmakers were more willing to embrace other entrants into the market because the internet was looking like it would be the next evolution in car media. And within this there were forums where readers/consumers could discuss what they liked or didn't like. My name seemed to crop up a bit, and I was beginning to feel aggrieved that I was sustaining or building brands for business owners who didn't pay great money, and I had no equity in those brands. I think as foot soldiers none of us has the right to expect any type of ownership, but when magazines start plonking your name on the cover because they think it will sell more copies, perhaps that relationship should change.

I was earning decent money, had a nice house in the country and my second child had just been born. But I didn't really see a clear path to the next step, and in your 30s and 40s you really should be looking for just that. Then my friend Richard Meaden rang and said he had an idea ...

SEVENTEEN
DRIVERS
REPUBLIC

Frustration is the carcinogen of the workplace. The human resources remit now probes so deeply into personal circumstances the process is muddied by all manner of other life issues, but I reckon most of the time the glum faces and lack of motivation come from people being frustrated in their role.

Much of that is rooted in disliking authority – a behaviour that appears to be growing exponentially as social and legal pressures effectively end the boss/subordinate dynamic. I loved being the subordinate because I saw it as a temporary time in life where I could learn how to be the boss. But I am also pretty bad at taking orders from people who I don't idolise, so that's why I went freelance very early in my career – I was only a staff member of *Autocar* for four years. At the time people thought I was insane, but it was possibly the wisest thing I've done because it taught me that the fear of failure isn't something any of us should consider when making big decisions. Exposing your loved ones to poverty? Yep, that's worth taking into account. Wrecking your mental health? Red-flag time. But don't be scared of failure.

If the first real risk I took on paper was going freelance, it wasn't really anything of the sort because I went into the great self-employed unknown with a contract that guaranteed enough money to live off. When I answered a call from my friend Richard Meaden in early 2008, I didn't have any of those securities. I've known Dickie (as he's known) since my first year as a journo. He was older than me and had been part of the founding crew of *evo* magazine; he was at the very top of his game as a driver and writer. He wanted another challenge and, like me, was succumbing to the frustration of no longer having equity in the brand he supported. We agreed that the time was right to produce an electronic product for the hardcore car community. He said he had a man who would financially back the idea, and we should meet.

We did just that. He was called Steve Davies, and at just about any other time in my working life, after that meeting, I'd probably have said to Dickie, 'This is the right thing to do, but Steve isn't the right person to do it with.'

But I didn't think that at all at the time, despite some pretty obvious signs that we would find it hard to work together. I thought we were going to shake up our industry, and once we became infected with that zealous desire to execute an idea we felt was game-changing, we didn't slow down and take stock. We just barrelled on with zero fucks given. And that's what makes episodes like Drivers Republic so important. It nearly ruined me financially and emotionally. But would I change any of it? Probably not. I suppose it's a bit like your first boyfriend/girlfriend experience: you're so drunk with excitement that nothing else matters. And the one thing you don't feel when you embark on potentially ruinous business ventures is the frustration of being subordinate.

So Drivers Republic was born when Dickie Meaden, Jethro Bovingdon and Neil Carey left *evo* and I left *Autocar*. Steve Davies was a management consultant with some cash to spend and Allan Pattison was the man who would sell the idea to car brands. The modest aim was to become Facebook for cars. Back in 2008 everyone figured they could crack their vertical within the media by building a community and then buying yachts and expensive racing cars on the proceeds of guiding those eyeballs through a web of big-spending car brands. As far as I'm aware not one of them made it to profitability, let alone survived.

In the spring of 2008 we soft-launched the product by releasing some videos, using a new outlet called 'Twitter' and generally making as much noise as possible. Nothing about who owned what was, to my knowledge, ever written down and we ploughed on, building a website and getting higher on our own supply. A website called PistonHeads had emerged as a motoring phenomenon at that time – its mixture of forums and classifieds was hugely popular. The traffic it generated dwarfed anything a print product could offer and it had just been bought by Haymarket – the company that owned *Autocar*, the magazine I had just left. Looking back, it was all very complicated, with many people who had long histories being thrust into new rivalries that had the potential to go wrong.

Thinking about it now makes me realise how strange the world of motoring journalism was. The pool of people who held the desirable roles on the car magazines, or actually got to drive and review the stuff that you really wanted to experience, was tiny. And because we all shared a passion for the subject and ended up at the events where these cars were launched, most of us became pals. Not bezzie mates, but decent friends. But we were also genuine rivals – that's actually a strange dynamic, and not one I've experienced since.

Suffused with our childish, blind positivity, we set off to sell our new e-magazine and car community business to the car companies themselves – most of whom were quite receptive. We needed access to as many new car launches as possible and the telephone numbers of their respective advertising agencies. The timing seemed right for the switch to digital media – there were just two slight issues. It was clear fairly early on that I could not fathom much of the way Steve viewed the world, and some of my clever friends who made lots of money told me that the economy might soon be in a spot of bother. Oh, and we were not paying ourselves anything.

Through the summer of 2008 we built the site and then launched it with as much content as possible. The main sell to the carmakers was that being a community – and members therefore having to share information about themselves – the conversation would be more positive, as opposed to forums like PistonHeads which was already becoming contaminated by faceless gobshites.

The launch was successful, we created some content I'm still proud of and even though the community was tricky to grow it did begin to rumble along well enough for us to open commercial conversations with many car brands about sponsorship and advertising on the site. And then on 9 September a bank called Lehman Brothers announced it was 'facing difficulties' and its stock dropped 45 per cent. The next week all but two of the car companies with whom we had outline commercial agreements told us that they were dropping out. We should have shut the doors there and then.

But of course we didn't. We doubled down and decided that despite the fact people were queuing to withdraw cash from Northern Rock, our little website was not only going to weather the storm, but it would emerge and vanquish the antiquated print media. God knows what we were smoking, but what happened over the next year was utter madness.

It very quickly became us against Steve. I know I acted against my better instincts to go ahead with him, and it was a very tough life lesson. However, the harshest situations are often the funniest because, on reflection, you simply cannot believe the absurdity of what you landed yourself in.

We had a small office in Blisworth, close to the Silverstone circuit (not exactly handy if you live near Monmouth) and from the moment Lehman went pop, working life was a struggle. Neil, Jethro and Dickie would be in the office most days, and I'd try and be there a few times a week – a situation that was only really affordable because the lovely Rob Halloway of Mercedes-Benz lent me a W211 E320 CDI estate and then applied a cheeky Brabus remap, so I could pump along at an indecent lick and still achieve 36mpg.

The first stark reality of producing content when there is very little income is that you automatically revert to the line of least resistance. All those grand plans of gorgeous features remembering the heroes of yesteryear are dropped straight into the bin when BMW phones and offers you a slot on the new 320d launch event because it's cheap and you'll get a few internet page impressions to boast about to the next potential client.

And earning no money is utterly corrosive. We often think that the best way to demonstrate our commitment to an organisation or a process is to say, 'Don't worry about paying me just yet,' but in doing that we set ourselves on an inevitable path of unhappiness and conflict. When times are good, anyone can look in the mirror and say they're okay earning nothing on a promise, but the moment the wind changes direction you have yourself a huge mess. Conflicts that might have been resolved become much trickier – the workplace becomes the perfect breeding ground for resentment.

And so I became massively resentful of Steve and what I thought was his unrealistic outlook on everything, and of the fact that he decided to stop spending his own money on a project that clearly wasn't going to return anything like what he'd hoped in the first place. And that second part now seems completely reasonable to me, but at the time I felt strongly that he was going back on his commitment.

Office meetings very quickly became frosty affairs where Steve would say things that we didn't agree with and we'd just roll our eyes. Then they descended into silliness when Neil's dog Gwyndaff would scratch around and sniff for a you-know-what as we discussed the dire state of the business. I think it was around that time that Jethro went to sign on for tax credits driving a press Lamborghini.

The work experience lads were a highlight too. One chap was called Pete, and during his lunch hour he'd watch films on his laptop entitled 'cake fart'. I had never seen anything like that before, and I don't want to again. He was incredibly keen, which is what we all want in a workie, and once drove a car all the way to the south of France to meet me for the launch of the Ford Mk2 Focus RS. The only problem was, shamefully, I don't think we'd given him any cash and from memory his mobile phone ran out of credit. We completely lost him, and I think found him by chance on some mountain pass.

The photographer was the legendary Kenny P, a man who once did a lap of the Nürburgring facing the wrong way riding pillion on a motorcycle to get a tracking shot. He was lurking in the bushes to get a panning shot of the Ford when I saw him suddenly bolt and run towards the road, then over the road and into field on the other side – a large wild boar was a few inches away from his backside. Kenny could really shift when he needed to.

CHAPTER SEVENTEEN

I think 2009 might have been the nadir of the motor car. Most car lovers felt the game was up, that there was no future in enjoying motoring or fast machinery. Honda was so spooked it gave us the weird hybrid CR-Z – remember that? At that Focus RS launch event in France the head of comms for Ford Europe told us all we should enjoy it, because Ford would never make a car like that again, in fact most carmakers wouldn't. Thank God he couldn't have been more wrong.

The other work experience chap we had for a few weeks I called Robbie. He was bright and helpful. On his last day I said, 'Goodbye and thank you, Robbie,' and he said, 'My name is Mark.' Sorry, Mark – I think my brain was melting by then.

I think by the spring of 2009 we were in a state of open warfare with Steve. We'd worked out that he could probably read all of our email conversations because he'd set up the accounts (not that I'm sure he ever did), so we would ping messages saying, 'Move to covert email', and other such nonsense. We tried to find outside investment so we could buy him out and we also tried to find a buyer, but of course there wasn't really anything to sell.

Come summer, we didn't have any money at all, and personally I was living in a fantasy land. I'd taken equity from the family home, I was underwriting our editorial activities more than any of the others and to compound the utter madness I bought a used Ferrari 612 Scaglietti on the skinniest finance deal imaginable. That was the last money I had, and rather than do something sensible with it I bought a sodding Ferrari. The nearside front tyre sprang a slow puncture soon after I took delivery and because a new one was £300 or so I just kept an old-fashioned footpump in the passenger footwell and would reinflate when necessary. Onlookers were bewildered. It was all quite pathetic, and I should have just stopped and sought professional help.

It all finally went wrong in July. We hadn't been producing any content, communication with Steve had ended (I think he'd fired us all, or some such nonsense), so I did what I always do when my head is frazzled and I want to escape life – I blagged a free ticket to the cricket. It was England vs Australia at Lord's. The last thing I remember about that day before I drank as much booze as I could was that my favourite cricket player finally took five wickets at Lord's and delivered one of his famous stigmata celebrations – Andrew Flintoff.

There were some other utterly Laurel and Hardy performances as Drivers Republic terminally unwound – people removed computer equipment from the office and then changed the locks, and a pair of Subaru Imprezas which I think were due to be given away in a competition became the subject of a police search, but I really can't remember all the details.

What I do recall is the desolate feeling of failure. A group of us had given up what must have been the best salaried jobs in motoring journalism. We had tried to take on and usurp the places that had previously given us work, and I think to many we had been left looking foolish. Perhaps some people respected the fact we'd tried, and from my side I think I left enough doors open that there was a chance to slide back into being a normal freelance journalist.

The mental and financial side-effects of that year took much longer to heal. I was listless and unmotivated, I didn't really want to be testing cars – in fact I fell out of love with cars for a while because I saw them as something that had led me down a path of near self-destruction.

Good things do emerge from rotten situations, though. I knew there was an audience that liked my work. It felt like there might be an emerging appetite for a type of sub-*Top-Gear* video style aimed at nerdier folk and it might be a possible career path – YouTube was growing quickly. But I still didn't have any work. Then Harry Metcalfe, the founder of *evo* magazine phoned and asked if I fancied coming to work there. His magazine was easily the most directly affected by Drivers Republic, but he wasn't about to dwell on that and he also saw the same video opportunity I did. So I agreed to go and work at *evo*.

But the best thing about Drivers Republic was that I worked with a chap called Neil Carey. He was the art editor of *evo* and made DR look quite stunning. It would take a couple of years, but Neil would be instrumental in shaping the next part of my working life. And the other boys? We all whinged for a while about Steve and the situation we found ourselves in and then, like me, they just shuffled off to whatever work was available. On the odd occasion we're in the same room, the whole episode makes us smile.

EIGHTEEN
EVO AND BEYOND

Life at *evo* was good fun. In some ways it felt like Drivers Republic had never happened, as if that weird year was just an unfortunate and slightly embarrassing kink in the space–time continuum and I went back to being the bloke who drove supercars for other people and wrote about them.

It wasn't quite as straightforward as that because, as mentioned, the strange paradox of friendship and competitor existed here, but I was on the wrong side of it this time. I didn't have many allies on team *evo* and my arrival landed like a wasp in a can of Fanta. Yes, I can be too loud, and I completely understand if that puts people off, but the *evo* office in 2009 was like a morgue. The first job I did was join the team for the annual ECOTY (*evo* Car of the Year) event. For those of you who aren't car magazine saddos, this was and is a gathering of the best fast cars of the year, adjudicated on by a load of people like me, who drive them all on great roads and sometimes a circuit, then decide on a winner. It's hard to think of anything more fun for car nerds.

In 2009 this was happening on the Isle of Skye. Although the weather was unhelpful, the scenery was knockout, and I remember thinking not just how lucky I was to be driving these cars but how much the average reader of *evo* would love to be here enjoying the same experience. But the sad reality was that none of the *evo* crew seemed to have much fun – mealtimes were stagnant affairs where people whinged about how *evo* wasn't what it used to be (subtle dig!), and then engaged in the type of conversation that made it sound as if everyone's fascinating week at home had been ruined by being dragged to Skye. It was all a bit embarrassing.

I think the second job I did for *evo* was the launch of the Ferrari 458. This was a huge step up from the old 430, and even at the time it felt like Ferrari had moved the game on in a way that rivals would struggle to match. Ferrari new product events have always been a complete bunfight, and this was no different. You're allowed just the right amount of track time to not be able to film anything meaningful, and just too little road time to be able to get out of Maranello (which couldn't be a worse place to celebrate such a car on film). That's why we all end up on the same sodding road after the Ponte Samone and you see the same corners in all the films. Normally I don't like giving away too many trade secrets, but the world and his bloody wife seem to go there now, so who cares.

Anyhow, we retuned back to the UK, edited the video into something vaguely usable and then posted it on the Dennis

Publishing media player. Back in those days publishing houses that were grappling with the idea of making money from videos genuinely thought that hosting it themselves was the only way forwards, so they could serve advertising inventory against the views and take all the coin. The problem is the *evo* media machine hadn't supported a video as popular as the 458, the host was charging a lot for each stream and the whole exercise ended up costing the company money. Once bitten ...

Around that time there was another brilliantly Italian Ferrari situation. I think David Vivian, one of the best writers to ever approach the subject of cars, had tested the new convertible California and the gearbox had failed while he was testing it. The company was unwilling, or maybe unable, to supply another car in the UK when *evo* wanted to compare it to rivals like the Mercedes SL. So Harry and the team found a company that had one for hire and used that instead.

The first-gen California isn't one of Ferrari's better efforts, and it might just be that the car wasn't the best example, but it didn't fare especially well and Maranello went nuts. And the one thing that you can guarantee when Ferrari spits the dummy is that there will be some random unintended consequence that can be used to amuse yourself.

In this instance it was the letter that Ferrari sent to *evo* – and other media outlets. The Maranello missive expressly forbade journalists from driving any current model from its production cars without the factory giving permission. The 'current model' bit was designed to sidestep the many journalists who had older Ferraris and clearly shouldn't be subjected to any such rules. The only issue here was that I still owned that 612 – and Ferrari was still knocking out a few. This meant, according to the new rules of engagement laid down by the Scuderia, that it was a 'current' model and I therefore needed to ask permission to drive my own car. Of course, being a complete child I did just that and, for a few weeks, every time I'd finished pumping up that front tyre, I'd call the main reception at Ferrari and ask if I could go and buy a loaf of bread. To which they would ask, 'What?' And after a while they'd just hang up.

But *evo* did become more fun. Dickie Meaden did some freelance so we could have a laugh, and the editor Nick Trott was a decent chap. But it just wasn't my home. Origins matter in the workplace. I could have worked at *evo* for a decade and I'd have still felt more at home after one day in the *Autocar* office. Some of the above might have been a legitimate whinge at how flat the place was but actually the tribal side of life is exactly the way I like it. I'd been the enemy two years earlier – just because Harry had offered me a job doesn't mean the others shouldn't be allowed to have their noses put out of joint because some gobby little frog from *Autocar* has rocked up and is driving all the flash cars.

The other issue was trickier. I was spending a lot of time travelling – that in itself wasn't unusual – but for the first time I tended to be doing it with people I didn't know that well or just wasn't that friendly with. My working life has been one of travel and experiences that I can't really comprehend sitting here in Bristol typing, but if there's one regret it's that all too often I ended up in the right situation with the wrong person. I wish I could have shared those moments with my closest friends or loved ones.

About a year into working at *evo* I was filming at Lamborghini and for whatever reason we couldn't make the flight home. These were the days when Lambo wasn't run by berks in tight-fitting suits, and they very kindly said, 'Stay here for the night and go to this place for a meal.'

Sant'Agata is near Bologna, a foodie high point in the country that has the best food of all. And here I was sitting opposite a photographer who I got on okay with, but nothing more. We ate the most delicious meal in silence, like we had done on the previous five jobs, and it all felt like a bit of a waste to me. Then we couldn't get a cab back to the hotel, which was only a slight problem because I'd spotted Lamborghini test-driving legend Valentino Balboni sitting with his family on the way in and said hello. He then saw us lurking nervously and said he'd run us home.

But Valentino didn't have anything other than a Balboni Edition Lambo Gallardo in which to take us back, and that meant shuttling us individually and interrupting his family meal. It was only a five-minute drive, but he gave it plenty of tap and I thought it the most perfect end to the most perfect random Italian evening. The photographer received the same ride home but wasn't really interested. How much would someone like me pay to have Valentino drive me home in that manner, in Lamborghini's home town? Had Lamborghini actually set up the whole thing? Answers: quite a lot, and yes

– quite possibly. But who cares? Experiences aren't complete unless you have someone to celebrate them with.

And so life rumbled on. *Evo* was fine, but despite having some sort of revenue share on the video side, that clearly wasn't going to burp anything meaningful if the company was losing money hosting videos that did decent numbers. The main upside was that the financial collapse of 2008 already seemed like a distant memory and people decided that the phrase 'quantitative easing' meant 'cheap loans to buy cars with'.

The fast-car scene exploded as quickly as we had feared it might die. Porsche gave us a 997 GT3 with a 3.8-litre engine, then an RS and a GT2 RS. Mercedes launched a proper modern-day gullwing called the SLS and BMW was still pumping out M cars. Without realising it, I think we were just heading into the greatest period in the history of fast road cars. Two of them, the 997 GT2 RS and the SLS, were involved in one of the more fortunate escapes of my driving career.

And that does bring me neatly to the thorny issue of shunts and near-misses. The culture of sharing the things that go wrong in cars when driving them is your day job couldn't be more different now than it was twenty-five years ago. Then, it was a case of do anything to cover up any shunt. Now it's not only a case of ramping up the clickbait drama to the point of being completely disingenuous ('I crash my new Lamborghini!!!' – only you watch the vid and see no such thing happen) but actively manufacturing situations where you make accidents occur, so you can film them and get more views.

If you wanted a single snapshot of why my generation finds the Gen-Z YouTube world so confusing, that's it right there. We hid it, they shout about it.

Given my position on this you won't be surprised to learn that I'm not about to spill the beans on all of the crashes I've had. There have been a few. No one's perfect, and some of them I'm not very proud of. Some were genuinely funny. But the closest I've come to ending up in the newspapers was probably on a Yorkshire moor, driving a 997 GT2 RS. The name Dickie Meaden is also involved.

This was *evo* Car of the Year 2010 – I think. I am driving the aforementioned Porsche and Richard is in the Mercedes. We're heading up and down a brilliant piece of moorland A-road that is well sighted with no hedges, and a pair of photographers are snapping away merrily and all is good with the world. There's a crest that, above a speed I won't type here, becomes a neat little jump and one of the joys of still photography is that a skilled snapper can make even the slightest leap look majestic in a way that would seem unremarkable to the naked eye on a video. But this is 2010, and something called the GoPro camera has just emerged and is altering the way we film cars. As Dickie and myself drive up and down this road, there's one on the rear of the SLS facing back to the following Porsche and one on the front of the Porsche looking at the sexy rump of that Merc.

I'm following at a safe distance. There is a blind point when I come over the crest after the Merc, but we've done several runs and Dickie is a long way up the road when I can see clearly. And then on the next run I arrive, and where there had been the most inviting, comforting rasher of road wriggling into the distance, there is an SLS braking very hard, in the middle of the road, with several sheep casually walking across. Point of fact: there is not a single situation in life where a sheep is helpful. Especially if you film cars for a living.

My closing speed is far too great for me to even consider being able to stop so I have to make a choice. My brain says jink right, but just as that thought is processed, the Merc heads right to avoid an especially obstinate fluffy ruminant attempting to stare down the long nose of the Benz. Left it is then. Precisely where I really don't want to go.

Left is heading off the road. There is bracken and low-lying shrubbery hiding whatever rocky nightmares might lurk underneath. I can remember heading off into that scrub thinking, 'I've always driven along here and thought to myself I really wouldn't want to end up in that shite carrying any kind of speed whatsoever.'

It all happened so damn quickly, but the more time you spend doing this driving stuff, the more these events seem to slow down as they evolve, and you're left making decisions far more quickly than you thought you were capable of doing so. I can remember heading into the doobies aware that the primary reaction was 'this is going to roll,' and then when both axles did in fact continue on the same trajectory being aware that I had one chance to try and steer the car back on to the road. I took that chance and the car made it back to the tarmac. The problem being that I had rattled it over a few hundred metres of terrain which was quite unsuitable for a machine designed to lap the Nürburgring. The call to Porsche wasn't much fun, but the other possible outcomes probably weren't worth thinking about. The underside of the GT2 looked like a war zone.

Should we ever glorify these events? Am I completely irresponsible telling you what happened that day, and in doing so should I be allowed to add a bit of flowery prose to make the thing seem like a casual yarn? I don't really have any answers for that. But I suppose I have in place a basic check system for what I think is and isn't fair game. I was on a moorland road in the middle of nowhere, and 13 years have elapsed since it happened. I'm not trying to glamourise the events, nor am I trying to absolve myself of any blame. And if anyone attempted to conflate those few paragraphs with some of the lunacy that's now on YouTube and appears to be completely ignored by the police, then I'd have two words for them – the second would be 'off'.

By 2011 I was probably a bit frustrated with *evo* and arriving at a similar mental space to the pre-DR time. Why am I building someone else's brand for them? Couple of differences this time, though: the memory of nearly bankrupting myself meant I was far less gung-ho about the possibility of making any new venture stick, and it seemed to me that in the UK, of all the electronic motoring media platforms, only PistonHeads was making any real money. And there were some juicy upsides coming my way from being at *evo*. The best, by far, was getting to know Andreas Preuninger at Porsche and having the chance to compete at the Nürburgring 24-hrs in a factory-entered Porsche.

I'd been racing there for many years by this point and with my friend Chris Cooper back in 2002 had somehow managed to drag a Caterham Seven over the line in 11th place overall, in a field of well over 100 cars. The following year the German race authorities banned Caterhams because we'd been too fast. A badge of honour to celebrate.

Subsequent to that I'd been doing as much racing as I could, but I always enjoyed driving at the Nürburgring more than other circuits, despite the obvious dangers. From 2007 myself, Chris Cooper and Guy Spurr raced with Team Parker Racing in a race series at the Nürburgring that couldn't sound more German if it tried – the Veranstaltergemeinschaft Langstreckenpokal Nürburgring. Luckily it was abbreviated to VLN. It was a series of mostly four-hour races that supported the blue riband 24-hr event. Frankly, any race there is awesome.

Chris and Guy owned the latest Porsche Cup racing car and I was allowed to drive it with them. We had many years of racing over there, for which I paid not one penny. I also roped in a genius suspension engineer called Graham Gleeson whose company EXE-TC had won nine world championships with Sébastien Loeb. We were competitive and I just loved those race weekends. But come 2011, Porsche offered me a chance to compete in the 24-hr race in a street-legal 997 GT3 RS 3.8. It was a fabulous journalistic opportunity because it evoked endurance racing of old by attempting to drive a road-registered car to the circuit, compete, and then drive it home.

Chris and Guy kindly let me do the two VLN practice rounds required by Porsche and the main event. Chris did call me a 'quisling', which I had to google.

You might be aware that I am a Porsche tragic – it is my favourite car company by far. When this life thing comes to a close and someone asks me which event would have made the 17-year-old me grin the most, having a Porsche factory contract to race a 911 at the Nürburgring or presenting *Top Gear*, the BBC won't get a look in. Late Spring 2011 was a dream. I even went running and became fit and did all sorts of things I wouldn't normally do because I didn't want to balls it all up.

My team-mates were Horst von Saurma, Patrick Simon and Roland Asch. Walter Röhrl was supposed to be in the car too, but he goosed his back a month before the big race. Come the event, the 997 RS was so good it almost made for a non-story because so little went wrong. The car drove to the race, came a scarcely believable 13th overall, beating a heap of specialised racing cars and the next morning was driven back to the factory in Zuffenhausen, where it is still in the museum. It was a dream come true for me. I still have the overalls and boots.

Completing the race wasn't the most important thing that happened to me at the Nürburgring 24-hrs in 2011. A few days before the race, a young American chap came up to me and introduced himself in the paddock. He was called JF Musial and was making a film for Porsche or some US network. You speak to hundreds of people at those events, and I simply cannot remember names, but he was so enthusiastic that the face and the name stuck. He mentioned something about YouTube during our brief conversation, but it didn't even register. A few weeks later he messaged: 'I'm serious, I have budget from YouTube to build a channel of car content and do you want to have a show on it?'

NINETEEN
DRIVE

John-Francis Musial was about 22 when he opened that conversation about YouTube. Had I known his age back then, events might have taken a different direction. I think we were sitting in a bar in New York the following summer when it dawned on me that I should ask him how old he was. Everyone seems more mature than me, but having an early-20-something clearly being much more capable at life stuck in the craw a bit. But then we were riding high on a YouTube channel launched six months earlier that everyone in our world was talking about. Fast forward a few years from that point and of the three stakeholders in that YouTube channel, one would be running a large production company, one would be presenting *Top Gear*, and one would be in prison.

That phone call with JF after the N24 quickly moved into some more concrete emails. He told me that YouTube was about to self-fund a load of individual verticals, one of them was automotive, and – the really important bit – the aim was to try and increase the quality of the content and persuade advertisers to spend more around quality. This was a pivotal time in the history of the world's largest video-streaming service – and you probably already know which way it went. But fair play to YT – it wanted to see if it could challenge conventional broadcasters and see whether there was any way of differentiating between the advertising spend around a cat standing on a skateboard, filmed on an iPhone, and a lovingly crafted short film. Apparently the fighting fund was over $100m, and JF had secured a little slice of it.

Sitting here now, I'm trying to identify some semblance of hesitance that must have nagged at the time, but I can't honestly say that I can recall anything like that. Life is a series of serendipitous opportunities that arrive at our feet – I was restless at *evo* and something very interesting was being offered as a next stage. The only test I felt I needed to apply was to understand the type of people I'd be dealing with, because I genuinely didn't know any of them. JF had mentioned Matt Farah, who I'd heard of; a chap called Alex Roy, whose sartorial Gumball activities had made me smile; and Mike Spinelli, who had founded the quirky Gawker Media automotive outpost called Jalopnik. But I hadn't shared a beer with any of them.

So I did something very juvenile – that I don't regret. As JF used all the US contractual language that makes me retch, like 'heads-of-terms' and 'your attorney', I just said to him: 'I'm racing at the Nürburgring in a few weeks' time, if you appear in person with a contract, I'll sign it.' He lived in New York at the time.

I was an inveterate blagger back then and used to borrow whatever I could to drive to VLN races. Not just to save money on depreciation (old journo habits die hard), but because the drive to the Nordschleife covers every possible driving scenario – it's perhaps the only test route any car tester needs. And that includes not driving the car around the track, as most road cars have no place being driven around there. This time I was driving a Bentley Mulsanne. It was burgundy and magnificent. I adore these massive old crocks and ended up owning one a few years later. They are one of the best value cars on sale if we apply a sensible interpretation of what that phrase actually means – the number of man hours and development £s that is invested in a machine versus what you have to pay for one now. A true bargain.

On the Friday morning of that race weekend JF sent me a text message – 'I'll be at the track for about 5pm – where will you be?' I gave him a location, still not believing for one minute he would appear. Sure enough, he arrived with a piece of paper. We sat in the back of the Bentley, in the car park for the tourist driving area of the circuit, shook hands and I signed that piece of paper. It was only when he said he had to dash back to the airport that it dawned on me he had flown over just to hand over that contract. If anyone is willing to do that, then they're worth working with.

The problem now was how best to capture as many eyeballs for these videos as possible. As previously mentioned,

PistonHeads was by far and away the biggest online destination for cars in the UK. I took advantage of the fact that, despite ruffling a few feathers with Drivers Republic, I still had a decent line of communication with Stuart Forrest, the Publisher of PH, and tried to sell him the idea of showcasing these new videos on his site, but them not owning the content. It was another one of those 'right moment' events, because PH was never going to spend the money creating those films, but they could pay for some words to accompany the embedded YT video player. We did a deal that I think worked for both parties.

Harry wasn't especially pleased with the news, but the rest of the *evo* team didn't seem too disappointed! I was worried, though – this wasn't a DR-sized risk, but I was leaping between brands again, and there's only so many times you can do that before people grow uneasy. Strangely, it was that year's ECOTY that reassured me that leaving *evo* was the right thing to do.

The plan was an ambitious one – get a load of cars shipped down to Portimão circuit on the Algarve, film them on the road and then spend some time on the fabulous new track. Another dream ticket. The slight problem being that the track-time negotiation had been slightly lost in translation. We had been granted a couple of hours in the gloaming after the track was closed. It was a shambles.

The local government had just completed a network of access roads to some car parks and a hotel that was being built behind the circuit. They were twisty and smooth, but deep drainage gullies ran alongside them. This was the only place we could realistically film, and if you got it even marginally wrong the car would be destroyed. We'd gone all the way to Portugal to drive around a hazardous car park. Oh, and on the day we arrived one of the crew had a massive stack in a C63 coupé, only two details of which I can still remember – that the car was a write-off, and the poor sod who crashed it had a three-pointed-star tattoo where the airbag had branded him. If I wanted to make films, I needed to not be at *evo*.

A production budget for 2012 films on YouTube was agreed. I think it was £144,000, and with this money I would have to deliver one film a week. That seemed a colossal amount of cash then, but wouldn't get you 20 minutes of *Top Gear* today. We were being audited on the number of hours of programming we delivered, so I think each film had to be ten minutes long. The channel was called DRIVE. My show was called *Chris Harris on Cars*. Everyone else on the channel went for generic show names, but this was a shop-window opportunity, and you need your name up there somewhere!

The next job was to find a cameraman. Obviously I'd made a few films before – starting all the way back at *Autocar* in 2006 with a series called 'Chris on Camera' (namechecking myself does begin to look like an issue now), and then there was DR and latterly *evo*. I'd worked with many talented professional filmmakers and went and saw each of them, but I couldn't quite see how it would work. This would be a bruising schedule, and they were gentle creatives. Anyhow – I had to deliver the first film on 11 January 2012, so I asked a chap called David Litchfield to come and film at Millbrook.

The idea was to take a very modern powerful AMG and stick it on a set of space saver tyres – those skinny things that protect boot space but can only do 50mph. This was a very good idea for a film, only it wasn't my idea. Rob Halloway from Merc had said to me, 'I wonder what it would look like, if …' and it turns out he was a creative genius. This is the man who once had to quietly sit in the passenger seat of one his precious AMG press cars as a Belgian policeman screamed at me: 'The limit is 130 kilometres an hour, not miles an hour.'

That video was transformative – the audience loved it. It established in my head a space where I could create films that would nourish my geeky audience and potentially spread beyond that, but I would completely avoid the accusation of being a pound-shop *Top Gear*. That last point was of paramount importance for me because *TG* was at its peak back then, and woe betide anyone who attempted to imitate it. The YT stats on the film were excellent, the PistonHeads audience liked it, the bosses were happy and all was dandy. I think the following week we put out a Ford RS200 and Audi Sport Quattro film which didn't quite match the C63 numbers, but the momentum was good and the fact we were revisiting older heroes sat well with people. Most of all, I was being allowed to film what I wanted – and that was so liberating. Predictably, three weeks into finally making something work, it all nearly ended.

If someone offers you the chance to film a McLaren F1, you don't stop and ask questions. My friend Edward Lovett had bought an F1 race car from Japan and was about to sell it in the UK – he thought a little video would help that process. To give you an idea of how much these have increased in price over the past decade, this one was around £1.3m in 2012 – they are now worth well over £20m. I wasn't allowed to drive it, but would sit in the passenger seat. There hadn't been any decent Macca F1 content for years, and some V12 noise coupled with me squeaking from one of the passenger seats would surely capture some eyeballs.

The day itself wasn't especially smooth. This was a racing car with number plates – or rather trade plates. It had a full Lark race livery and was fractionally quieter than Concorde. Sensibly, we decided to film it in and around Swindon, where a police car lurked around every corner. There was no passenger seat, so I just wedged myself into one of the spaces that might have been one in a road version of the F1 and held on to the roll cage. Obviously there was no seat belt. Edward occasionally gave it the berries and I occasionally asked him to slow down a bit. After one especially muscular and tattooed police officer had finally had enough of us, the car was taken back to Dick Lovett HQ.

The film went live the following week, and the numbers were astonishing. It was tracking at double the volume of the C63 effort and it was being discussed everywhere – mostly for the wrong reasons. That film was a big error of judgement from me – of the type I hadn't made before, nor have I really made since. I suppose it was my closest flirtation with an early form of clickbait – not because I was trying to dupe an audience into thinking a film contained content that wasn't there, but because I allowed my head to be seduced by the promise of views over what I knew was acceptable or damaging to me or those around me. No one would bat an eyelid at that type of indiscretion now, but people did in 2012. Including the police and the Dick Lovett business.

So as the film accrued big numbers and JF and his YT overlords in the US loved the audience growth, someone from the police very kindly suggested that I should take the video down. And then someone from Dick Lovett suggested the same thing, but with a slightly more sinister tone of voice. I didn't much like any of this, so phoned JF and asked him to remove the F1 film, but he was under pressure to leave it there. For an afternoon I didn't know if I was going to be arrested by the cops or sued by Dick Lovett, or YouTube. It was hideous, entirely of my own making, and I can see why that dealer group felt a degree of reputational damage. YouTube did relent, it was removed, and I apologised to all involved. Never again.

The other lesson I learnt during that episode was that nothing is ever fully deleted from the internet. Someone rips it and hosts it where you can't control it. In this case it ended up on some Chinese site, but also on people's personal computers. That was my first exposure to the real nastiness of a place like PH – some people who had stolen that YT video from my channel took great pleasure in suggesting that if it would help the police they would post it again.

Those first few films were made by Dave Litchfield and a few other people, but the work process wasn't sustainable – I'd approached the problem from the wrong perspective by

RHD 993 GT2. Sold for £130,000 in 2007. Now worth well over a million. Balls.

997 GT3 3.6. Use and abuse is the only way I know.

Racing when
I had hair.

Working with
Nigel Mansell.
He'll always be
one of my heroes.

The infamous
McLaren F1 film
with Edward Lovett.

Lister Costin Coupe at the Goodwood Revival TT, 2013.

On the podium with Alex and Chris, Garage 59, 2018.

Everything looks better at Goodwood. Even me.

512 TR which I wish I'd never sold. Adored it.

Driving Morse's Mk2 Jag for *Top Gear*.

My E30 M3 Rally car. Really should use it more!

My Escort Mk2 gravel rally car.
Everyone should have one.

Andrew Flintoff on the roof
of a Bentley I'm driving.
Standard *Top Gear*.

Drifting a
Veyron, on a
wet French B
road, 2006.
Code brown.

With Paddy
McGuinness
and Andrew
Flintoff, filming
Top Gear.

Matt Le Blanc in my
2CV. Loved working on
Top Gear with him.

Paddy ensuring I have
no more children.

Iceland, mid-summer, midnight, joshing with JF Musial and Mike Spinelli.

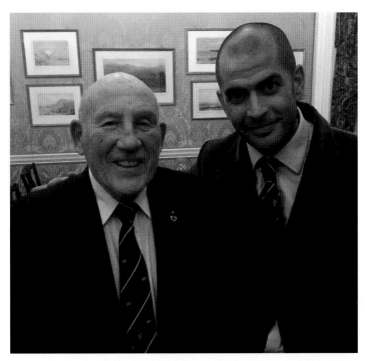

Meeting the man himself. Sir Stirling Moss. The racer's racer.

The late, and much missed Sabine Schmitz.

Downtime in Cornwall with my best mate Gazza.

Neil Carey and my dog Pip.

attempting to take a filmmaker and persuade them to come and make sense of my mad world and insane schedule. So I went and saw Neil Carey from DR and asked him if he fancied coming and making films. At this point Neil really hadn't made anything at all, but he has an eye for what looks good, he's willing to have a go at anything and, most importantly, I could easily see myself spending a lot of time with him and talking utter nonsense. Between 2012 and 2015 I spent more hours with Neil than any other human being – he was my surrogate husband.

With Neil on-board, filming was more fun, the views on our show grew and the DRIVE channel was building nicely too. But some frustration was growing as well, in the same old way, because the numbers clearly demonstrated that my show was contributing more than the others and yet I had no skin in the game. The ownership of DRIVE was opaque – I knew JF had a chunk, but there was another owner called Emil Rensing (real name, honestly) who was JF's business partner. I'm not a businessman and have little interest in the structure of these things, but I flew to New York in the summer of 2012 to understand why someone who didn't appear to do much on DRIVE owned a load of it, and yet I had nothing. To my great surprise, as I was about to launch into that monologue in a meeting room just off Times Square, in Viacom's absurdly huge office where Emil worked, he and JF said, 'Let's go thirds – split equally.' It was the easiest equity I'll ever acquire. All you clever people will now be nodding sagely at how dangerous a phrase that is to type.

JF didn't really speak to me about Emil much, but it was clear there were some legacy issues from their side. I didn't have any idea how the money was distributed between the different shows. I also had no idea that the headline sum given by YouTube to the channel had been given a healthy haircut by Emil because it was through his connections with people at YT that DRIVE existed in the first place. Now, I think anyone who facilitates should be allowed to play the middle-man and apply what we might call here an 'Emil tax', but this example was just plain greedy.

Furthermore, we had to renegotiate the production budget for 2013, and it became clear that what we viewed as a success wasn't received the same way by YouTube. In fact we were toiling away making a rod for our own backs by producing ever-more professional films across the whole channel and this was allowing YouTube to prove its hypothesis that you simply couldn't apply an inflated advertising rate card because someone had spent more money making a film. The unpalatable truth is, I suspect, DRIVE in its original format was already doomed before its first quarter was completed, we just hadn't been told. The 2013 budget was significantly less, so we had to drop several shows, and when our business partner went to apply his 'Emil tax', JF and I had to tussle with him.

Everyone thought DRIVE was flying. Publicly, it was crushing it for views and subscribers, but by December 2012 I knew the channel probably wasn't going to be sustainable because if YouTube cut us from the funding model, and all we had was the incoming advertising revenue for budget, it wouldn't cover the cost of a single flight. It was all rather depressing.

We muscled through 2013 with smiles on our faces and did make many films I'm proud of. Life was still good fun, and working with Neil-o was a lively mashup of oversteer and speaking to foreigners with the most absurd Welsh accent possible. It's the most intense period of time that I've worked with anyone – we were literally making films 24/7.

I think it reached a peak around the spring of that year when we attempted to link three launch events back-to-back in Spain and France. There was never a cross word – it really was fun – but we ended up lost, driving a Mercedes 190 SL from the Merc museum somewhere near Barcelona, and neither of us could see the funny side of it. It was shit-slow and wasn't going to make a film. That night we took something that made Ryanair look like Cathay Pacific back to Nice, from where we'd flown to Spain two days earlier. We were attempting to cram stuff into days to an extent that it became disorientating – largely because we had unwittingly become so high-functioning in our roles that we felt invincible.

We landed back in France completely knackered and had to take the bus between the two terminals at Nice airport – one of those buses that sits with its belly on the floor and had an access ramp for trolleys and wheelchairs. I was just standing, hanging from a strap, probably asking Neil to say Pirelli in a Merthyr Tydfil accent, when I heard a crash, felt a nasty pain in my legs and the lights went out. I regained consciousness quickly afterwards, and instead of seeing the caring face of my work buddy all I could see was him unable to breathe with laughter, the side of a wheelchair and some manic French sounds being shouted by the person on that chair. Neil still rates it as the funniest thing he saw in all those years. Apparently this old piratical-looking dude – complete with eye patch – decided to give his wheelchair the full beans on entering the bus and didn't much care that he ran me over in the process. I still have the dent in my shin bone.

The real upside to operating like that is a telepathic knowledge of how each other works, and when you're filming cars sliding around I cannot tell you how much of an advantage that is. Neil and I would attend car launches and because he knew I could slide the vehicle just where he needed it, and I knew he'd only need two passes (one for slow-mo, one for full speed), we could quickly move on to the next shot. By 2013 everyone wanted to make films on car launches, but we could do it faster than all of them, and that meant we left with more shots and Neil could make a better film. Then we could lobby that same car company, because our video had more views than the others, to give us more time to make a film at their next event. It was a relentless process, and I loved the hustle. I don't think I was better at it than anyone else, but, just like those early days at *Autocar*, we worked harder than all of them and it brought results. However, the underlying issue remained – YouTube wasn't a long-term bet.

I think JF managed to squeeze a few months more from YouTube, but the game was up around March 2014. We went out with a bang, though, with a film on the McLaren P1 that people still talk about today. It was the most viewed film we did during those two years; our audience loved it. By then I'd stopped reading any of the comments, deciding that if you allow yourself to bask in the glory of adulation, by the same token you must also absorb all the accompanying negativity. But I did read the comments on that film, and they were heart-breaking because I knew we were done, that DRIVE couldn't continue as was, and I was facing professional reboot number God-knows-what. It seemed very exhausting.

TWENTY
LISTLESS

What happened next was unpleasant. The DRIVE funding ended, and we had to decide whether to continue and find an investor/collaborator or buyer. Or to just ditch the thing and run. JF had made some good contacts with the larger US television networks, and we ended up making content for NBC to broadcast around its F1 coverage. Some of the profits from that could then be spent keeping the boat afloat online, but it wasn't a lasting solution. With pernicious timing, YouTube then announced a paywall function on the site.

And so came the great dilemma: shut the thing down or see if people would pay for it. There was only one precedent for this in 2014, and it was *The Times*, whose online offering had gone behind a paywall. There was no public data available, but I did some digging with people I knew and what surfaced was sobering – 99 per cent of the traffic was lost. News International had the resources to sit that one out – not to mention revenues from a print product – but we had nothing other than a bunch of very loyal subscribers who had no intention of paying for what they'd been enjoying.

We decided to try the paywall option. We knew it wouldn't work and of course it didn't. We had tried to sell the business to multiple potential buyers, and, for me, it was time to give up. A few times I found the conversations with JF difficult. I was spending more time talking to Mike Spinelli as well, who was always a calm influence. I was also very sad when Matt Farah, who I counted as an ally and still call a friend, recorded a podcast that threw a load of allegations that I'd wasted money on films and hastened the demise of DRIVE. That couldn't have been further from the truth. I earned less than Neil in the two years we made those films. Still, when things like DRIVE unravel, there's always some heated collateral, so at the time I didn't respond to any of it. And I can still enjoy many beers with Matt.

I just sat and looked at my computer screen for a while and thought about how to reboot. Again.

As I was doing that I received something very rare indeed – a text message from a man called Brian Scotto. He was previously the editor of a US car magazine I'd written for called *0–60*, but he was now better known as the creative juice behind the Ken Block Gymkhana series. He asked me if I wanted to go and watch the latest one being filmed in LA, and said they'd give me a few beer tokens if I did some filming. Any ride with Ken was special – I always felt privileged at the time, but now he's sadly passed away I really do thank my lucky stars.

The Gymkhana business model was especially interesting to me, because they were the only people releasing car content on YouTube and making money. The films were free to watch and supported by a fleet of sponsors who existed on pre-rolls, post-rolls and any piece of real estate available within the film. I suppose I went to LA that time partly out of listless self-pity, but also to try and understand how I might try and make the sponsorship method work. I came away pretty despondent: my game is reviewing cars and telling the truth about them. This means the one group of companies I simply can't take money from is the carmakers themselves – and they're the ones who have the most cash to spend. Sponsorship was going to be a hard game if I wanted to retain my ability to be banned by companies like Ferrari.

Ah, being banned. I've been banned from driving a few brands in my time – Ferrari, Lamborghini, Aston Martin, to name a few. And there are others. The great motoring journo Peter Robinson told me that being banned for the right reasons was a badge of honour, and I believe he's correct. There are a few vertebrates left in my world, but mostly it's just brown-nosing spineless influencers merely interested in being invited back for the next free weekend away. Sadly, I'm genetically programmed to be unable to avoid a fight, so one day I decided to have a pop at Ferrari.

The article was published on Jalopnik back in 2011. It wasn't meant to be deliberately sensational, I just felt that Ferrari's method of preparing cars for magazine and tele-vision tests had gone unchecked for so long that most of us, if scrutinised by the people who were consuming our reviews, would look pretty foolish. It was a creep in behaviour over a decade, with cars being 'optimised', large teams of technicians arriving with test cars and, at a very basic level, those factory Ferraris not feeling very similar to the cars that customers were buying. I called them out in a story, and Ferrari didn't go nuts like it normally would. It did something far more worrying – it stayed silent. Publicly, many people were talking about what I'd written, and they wanted to know why those things had been said. I suppose I wanted it to be a call-to-arms for my trade – which I've always been proud of – to say enough was enough. Of course, there was no solidarity! Just a load of motoring hacks who thought, 'That's one less competitor to worry about when it comes to getting invited to the next Ferrari launch!'

That whole saga festered for a while, and then towards the end of 2012 a man from Ferrari said he wanted to meet me in London to discuss the issue the Scuderia had with me. I really wasn't expecting that at all. So we met at a pub in Mayfair and he said he was utterly tired of fielding calls from people asking if there was any truth in the Jalopnik story I'd written, and that we should bury the hatchet and just get back to being as we were. This all sounded rather pleasant and I'm sure I was naive enough to allow myself to think Ferrari gave a single shit about me, but really this was just a man fed up with being asked the same question. We had a decent lunch, and he did that classic Ferrari thing of telling me the matter was closed and then immediately listing a raft of other issues they had with me. The upshot was a video from early 2013 of a 458 Spider sliding around Llandow circuit in Wales that meant I was back in the fold. A year later that conversation in the pub would probably prove career-changing.

I couldn't take money from car companies so I had to draw up a list of suppliers to the industry that wouldn't compromise all the stuff listed above. Tyres seemed the obvious thing, so I reached out to Pirelli and its motorsport boss Paul Hembery was very helpful. Then someone told me about a website called Patreon – a place where people could pay a monthly sum to creators.

And this was the plan for the end of 2014 and the whole of 2015. We'd rustle up some sponsorship, see what ad revenue YT could generate and then hopefully a few people would take pity on us and donate a few quid on Patreon. And that was the order in which I assumed the sums of money would fall. As ever, that was completely wrong. By the spring of 2015 we were mostly surviving on the generosity of Patreon and some cheeky commercial work that I think Neil and I felt was probably going to be the best way of making a living in the future. By commercial, I mean making films for car companies. Not anything that compromised me as a hack, just beautiful clips and images they could use as launch assets. I was settling into this new way of existing when my little world was turned upside down.

Firstly, Jeremy Clarkson publicly called out Ferrari for not giving *Top Gear* the new LaFerrari supercar so it could record a lap time at its test track. A few weeks later at the

CHAPTER TWENTY

Geneva Motor Show I was scrabbling around with only one goal: securing factory-backed versions of that Ferrari, the Porsche 918 and the McLaren P1. The history of my trade is defined by exploring rivalries and then trying to deliver the very best story/video or whatever the media may be on that subject. Everyone in my world was trying to get those three cars together, but I wasn't interested in some low-speed celebration, I wanted to take them to a track and answer the simple question all geeks wanted answering: What's fastest?

The respective motor show stands were all pretty close together. I went around them like I was shopping for tricky food ingredients – it was quite bizarre. Porsche first, as I had a good relationship with them, and they simply said, 'Tell us where and when.' McLaren were equally sanguine, and it really helped that the P1 film we'd shot the year before had gone down well. None of this really mattered if Ferrari didn't want to join the party. I'd asked several times to borrow a LaFerrari but they just said a flat 'no' to any comparison tests. I wandered onto the Ferrari stand and waited patiently to speak to the communications boss. I didn't bother with any pleasant-ries and just asked him what I'd probably asked for a month earlier. He paused, looked around, grinned, and said, 'Yes, okay, because it will piss off Clarkson.' That was the same man I had sat opposite in a Mayfair pub 14 months earlier.

This was the holy grail. This film would be big enough to set the channel on a different trajectory. I think Neil and I slunk off somewhere quiet and had a cup of tea. We didn't really believe what was happening. Then a week later the news broke that the BBC had suspended Jeremy for punching someone. That was the biggest news story my industry had ever witnessed. It was all quite a lot to absorb.

It sort of affected me, and yet it didn't. I've avoided talking about Jeremy so far because I don't really know how to approach him as a subject. As the new host of *Top Gear* I've just spent the last seven years trying not to antagonise him because he has some very powerful friends in the media and he could make my life very difficult indeed if he chose to. I've only spoken to him once, at the Carrera GT launch in 2004. How many people can claim to have become bigger than the industry they once worked in? Not many, but he can. He's the most entertaining motoring writer of all time, and without his genius *Top Gear* would have remained a strange BBC magazine show produced out of Pebble Mill that showcased the latest in Farah trouser fashion.

Once it became clear there was no way back to the BBC for Jeremy, many people asked me if I'd been approached to present the show, and that seemed ridiculous to me. To the extent that I wrote another long soapbox diatribe on Jalopnik at that time explaining not only how important a healthy *Top Gear* was to the wider health of the global car media, but also that anyone who threw their hat into the ring to replace those three needed their head examining. Be careful what thoughts you commit to words, people.

Anyhow, the whole fracas quietly slid away – the way all stories do. James May was no longer being interviewed outside his London house looking vexed, and the world went about its business. For myself and Neil that meant building towards the big 918/P1/LaFerrari film and cracking on with some of these commercial shoots that were helping to pay the bills.

There was also a project with Singer, the company that reimagines Porsche 911s. Mazen Fawaz, who is now the CEO, was keen to explore the idea of a very special Singer with a specification from the gods. We spent many hours with Rob Dickinson, the creative genius behind the Singer brand, trying to devise what that car should be. That process began in the paddock of the Bahrain Grand Prix in 2014 when we sat down with the Williams Formula One team and asked if they would like to help develop that car. By Spring 2015 we were in the California canyons benchmarking a variety of different 911s to try to understand how that car could feel. It was and is one of the best things I've ever been involved with, and the car is now known as the Singer DLS.

So I'd found a way of keeping myself busy. The Chris Harris on Cars YT Channel was wobbling along okay, Red Bull TV was working with me on a potential treatment for a car show, and there was Singer and some subterranean commercial video work. We were filming one of those projects in Spain one day in June when my telephone rang. 'Hello, it's Chris Evans here. You've probably heard, but I've just been given the *Top Gear* job and people told me I should give you a ring.' I hadn't read the news because I was in Spain, and I hadn't received a call like that before.

The major contents of that call I can't remember. I was no doubt too busy processing the fact that Chris Evans had just phoned me, but I do remember how it ended. After 20 minutes gassing about cars and him saying positive things about my films, he ended it with, 'But I'm not going to offer you a job.' Which seemed an odd way to sign off.

Anyhow, I carried on working, finished that shoot and tried to forget that phone call had ever occurred because to dwell on it would probably cause much confusion. I don't think I told many people it had happened – I just parked it at the back of my noggin for the quirky moment it was and moved on.

Two months later people within the friend/rival matrix began dropping cryptic hints that they'd been invited to screen-test for roles on *Top Gear*. Throughout the summer there had been all manner of speculation about who might be in contention, but none of those names it seems ever were. I hadn't received a call and just assumed that was that, but a few days later, while working in Japan with JF, someone did call and invite me to do a screen test.

Up until this point in my life, I had completed one screen test. Actually, make that two. The first was for a show called *Driven* which I think was broadcast on Channel 4 about 20 years ago. It's where Mike Brewer made a name for himself, and Jason Plato was his sidekick. It was the Jason Plato role that I went for, and the screen-test tape must have been dreadful; I have never summoned the courage to watch it back. A year or so later, Jon Bentley, who used to produce *Top Gear* back in the day, asked me to test for something – I can't honestly remember what – and it was a total shambles. I remember meeting in a country pub car park in a Lotus – him asking me to talk about the car and just standing there stammering a series of 'ers' and 'ums'. Both episodes were cringeworthy, but also confirmed that scripts are not my thing. I'm not very good at remembering them, I'm not much interested in saying what someone else has written (I know, I could just write them myself) and the past few years had confirmed that the more gonzo style of just switching on a camera, skidding the crap out of a car and jabbering stream-of-consciousness style suited me down to the ground. The *Top Gear* screen test was the complete opposite. It was mostly scripted.

I was sent a document for some in-car driving and then some studio links. The Red Bull TV show was moving quite quickly at this point and it was my priority because we were well beyond a screen-test situation, and I was flying out to LA that afternoon to continue filming a pilot.

The test car for the *Top Gear* driving bit was a Mercedes C63 estate. I sat in it waiting for the minicams chap to adjust his kit and tried to ask him about the Panasonic camera he was using. This was a bad move – in telly, I now know the talent isn't really allowed to be interested in the kit. But my previous three years had been all about the kit, and I genuinely wanted to know what he thought of the camera. He didn't engage. I also knew that when that model of camera was recording, you could see a red light, and it wasn't illuminated. Was it worth telling him that the light wasn't on? How much of a pillock would I look if the light was on and I couldn't see it? I've never thought so deeply about the illumination status of an LED. It worried me – so as politely as a man can ask a professional a deeply insulting question about his job, I asked, 'That is running, isn't it?' He didn't reply and walked away. *Top Gear* didn't seem very friendly at that point.

I got the scripted driving bit out of the way as quickly as possible, then tried to enjoy the ad-lib section they'd offered and slid the car around with a decent amount of precision. I can remember wanting to demonstrate that I could do all this and know how not to just immolate a set of rear tyres need-lessly. But none of the *TG* team appeared to care either way.

The studio section was as horrific as expected. That vast hangar housed the metal cage where the three amigos had created the biggest factual television show of all time, and we were using it as a prop for some trial links. It just felt macabre and wrong. As millions of you will no doubt have observed, I'd rather smear radioactive waste on my private parts than deliver studio links, so I just rattled through them and left. I think two people from *TG* said thank you, the others shuffled off to prepare for the next victim and I drove away confused as to how I should react.

On the one hand it hadn't been a disaster. This was a good thing. But being there and seeing the track and seeing that logo had weakened the self-protecting inner resolve I'd summoned to not care about the outcome of that screen test. I arrived genuinely ambivalent as to the outcome – I'd left knowing that I probably wanted the job. But it was done now and all I could do was drive to Heathrow and wait to hear from them. Then my phone rang. 'Hi, Chris, is there any chance you could pop back to the track, we've had a technical problem – the onboard camera for your driving section wasn't running and we need you to do it all again.' So I went back and did it all again – and asked the camera bloke if his camera was firing, again. Mr Cameraman seemed more contrite second time around.

It occurred to me recently that the whole thing might have been a setup to see how I reacted under pressure, but the *TG* chaos machine doesn't have the time to deploy such sophisticated traps.

Life trundled on for a month or so – I told very few people about that screen test. It lurked in the back of my mind and then I received an email saying I'd made it through an initial cut, and to await further correspondence. This duly came a few days later from Lisa Clark in a very polite note telling me that *Top Gear* had decided to move in a slightly different direction and they wouldn't be wanting me. Deep breath time, but no big meltdown. Just knowing I'd been good enough to be in contention was probably enough. Yes, I was gutted, but there were many other good things happening and I was determined to stay positive. The next day – no word of a lie – Red Bull phoned to say they were no longer interested in working with me. I drank some whisky after that call.

TWENTY-ONE
FORK IN THE ROAD

In the middle of turmoil you can still have the best time of your life.

Top Gear was done, Red Bull was done, the YT channel finances looked shakier than a Kashmiri ceasefire and, as usual, I was running out of money. None of this mattered though because Porsche, Ferrari and McLaren had agreed to give me their latest supercars! The ever-lovely Paulo from Portimão circuit had said we could film there for several days at zero cost and we were on our way.

I am the most disorganised man I have ever met. Actually, can you meet yourself? Good question, that. With me comes chaos and disorganisation on a special level, and everyone connected to my life loves telling people just how bad the situation is. Well, you naysayers, answer this – how did I manage to organise every single aspect of that Holy Trinity film?! I still think about how much went into that week. It was a logistical bowl of spaghetti, but we made it work. I've front-funded many films in my time – it's a very risky way of operating, and even when you back yourself there will always be a vestige of doubt that you'll ever stand a chance of recouping the cash. This was by far the most I'd ever spent – nearly £50k of my own money – but for once it never even occurred to me that it wouldn't be worth doing.

My pal Marino Franchitti came out to drive the cars, as did the legend Tiff Needell. Tiff had to arrive a day late because he'd been on the piss at some rugby match, and that rather set the tone for what I think was the most fun I've had filming a bunch of cars. We had control over what we were doing with no execs and directors getting in the way. We had Neil and the best stills photographer I've ever worked with, Jamie Lipman. We had Mavro, a genius Red Bull cameraman, fly in from the US and we just ensured every minute was fun. The driving, the filming, the attempting and failing to match Tiff on the red wine in the evenings – all of it was joyous. We'd all cram into this rented Mercedes Vito in the mornings and hammer up the once-brilliant road from the golf resort we were staying at to the circuit. Subsidence had left some massive bumps, and every morning one of them would catch Tiff out as he snoozed on the back row: 'Fucking stop doing that, Harris!'

Many things resonate from that week in Portugal and the film we produced. It gave me the confidence to realise that despite some tricky setbacks not only was there a way of continuing doing our own thing, filming like this and retaining control at all levels, but it protected us from the nastiness of the outside world. You can't feel broken and shattered if you don't allow outsiders into your world.

Another abiding memory is of the car most people had the least interest in – the Porsche 918. Firstly, I learnt that if someone parks a 918 for the night and the last thing it did before sleepy time was lap very fast, check that the brake pads haven't glazed over. One morning I went out and fiddled with a camera and then went full-bore into turn one at Portimão, and the brake pedal was just solid. Nothing happened. The car went straight on and through the gravel and stopped just short of the wall. I should have checked the brakes more rigorously, because we nearly didn't have a three-car film. But the image of the Porsche that will always stick with me is of walking past the McLaren garage with its tyres and technicians, then the Ferrari garage with even more of both, and then seeing the Porsche with one young bloke and a massive wheel brace. Turns out he was a just a work-experience kid. The company had so much confidence in the car they just sent it along like it was a cooking Boxster. How cool it that?

One other memory involved us filming the final sequence. It's just me, Marino and Tiff hooning the three cars around the circuit – sliding and dicing and doing exactly what we'd all do if presented with such an opportunity. At school you'd call it 'free-swim'. I was in the McLaren sliding as close to Tiff in the La Ferrari as I dared. Several corners from the end of the final lap of filming, the nearside rear wheel on the LaF started to move oddly. I could see the toe angle was changing and through one left-hander it looked like it might fall off. But

Tiff just stayed pinned to the throttle – all 1,000hp ripping chunks from that oscillating tyre. The onboard is wild – he's just hanging on for dear life. When he stopped, we found the top mount had completely sheared. How he'd not shunted was anyone's guess. Ferrari had been very relaxed about time that week, but suddenly became agitated. They said the car needed to be shipped back to the factory immediately to be fixed for the next test. I wasn't aware there was another test, until I saw Jeremy Clarkson post a photograph of the same three cars, at the same circuit, the following week. He and Mr Ferrari had clearly kissed and made up. Better get the film turned around quickly, then.

I knew we had a great film, conversations with new sponsors for the YT channel were brewing and this felt like a trajectory for a working life that could work. I spent the next month with Neil getting the Trinity film into shape and pursuing that direction. Then the BBC phoned to say they had changed their mind – they did want me to appear on the show. This was two months after they'd said they didn't want me. That's a confusing predicament.

This is how I tried to untangle it at the time. A large part of me wanted to roll my head back, chuckle like a maniac and say: 'So you put me through a genuinely hideous screen-test experience, left me hanging for a while, dropped me like a stone and now you've changed your mind? Get fucked. Oh, and that initial Chris Evans phone conversation was weird.'

But that's just inner bravado messing with your mind. What I was finding impossible to ignore was the concept of imagining how the 17-year-old me would answer that question. How can a man who was once the child that was handed a copy of *What Car?*, who memorised the 0–60 times of all the cars, not take the job on *Top Gear*? The urge is too irresistible – the notion of telling your 17-year-old self that you chose to not take the job of your dreams because you were butthurt and too proud is terrible and pathetic in equal measure. I told Alex I'd call him the next day with an answer – which of course was going to be yes. Eight years later, for all the experiences and people and cars, I'm still not sure if I made the correct call.

A deal was put to me that week – the first season of the new *Top Gear* would be eight episodes, and the BBC would pay me per episode. Let's just say the fee was not what I was expecting. Taking into account production schedules and all the other inertia that comes with television, I was taking a pay cut to leave my own two-bit internet car show and host the world's biggest car television show. That stung, and it shattered any sense that I might be able to look in the mirror and think that mine and my family's financial situation was sorted for life. I think a bit of me, a very foolish part of me, did in some way hope that might be the outcome of saying yes to the job. There was always open speculation about how much the others were paid, and I hoped some of that might land in my lap. I was 40 years old, tired, and much more skint than anyone close to me or a stranger to me could ever know. And this stung. Money has never motivated me. Not having to worry about money has always motivated me – the difference between those two states of mind is perilously close.

I set about unwinding many of the conversations I had been having to fund the YT channel. This meant some uncomfortable chats with individuals and businesses who had set aside budget to work with us. It also meant working with *TG*'s online team to secure some budget to make films for its YouTube channel and be able to keep Neil busy. Again, I wouldn't see a penny of that. The more I shut down all the hard work I'd done to become self-sufficient, the more I had nagging doubts about *Top Gear* and that maybe I should have stood up to that 17-year-old me and said, 'No way – you have to say no.'

And then it got worse, maybe because these things always have to. At this point I hadn't even met Chris Evans in person – I hadn't even been invited to go to the office, but I had verbally agreed to join the show. I got a call to say that Chris no longer wanted me in all of the first series; instead he wanted me in just four episodes. The payment schedule was pro rata: he'd just cut me in half. That was shattering. I dragged myself up to London to sign the contract with Adam Waddell, whose job title I still couldn't fathom when he left six years later. He was the money man, and he was probably having a better day than me.

Of course, I was sworn to secrecy at that point. November sailed by with very little contact. I had to ask if I could meet Chris to maybe talk about the show, but this clearly wasn't wanted. Eventually I pushed so hard I was told to go to his house in London where I sat on a sofa as he finished a production meeting, like a kid waiting to see the headmaster for a bollocking. The first thing he asked me was if I liked Caterhams, which was a rhetorical question because before I could wax lyrical about them he answered it himself and told me that he didn't get them at all. He wasn't interested in them. If I had to pinpoint the first moment when I thought I was in genuine trouble being a part of the new *Top Gear*, that was it. Anyone who loves cars understands the basic joy of a Caterham. It's like hearing a chef say they can't abide an omelette – it completely undermines their credentials as a passionate member of that community. I went back to Bristol even more despondent.

Having been told that I wouldn't be needed for filming until the new year I was then asked to film the new Ferrari F12tdf in the south of France. If anything is going to make you feel better about life it's a 780hp, rear-wheel drive Ferrari. But sadly, even that didn't help much. If the Holy Trinity shoot in Portugal registers as possibly the most enjoyable shoot I've experienced, that first *TG* film was the most miserable. There was no chat with the director and the script was infuriating because it was so clearly not my voice. How the hell can I sit here now and say that the BBC paid me to drive one of the most extreme road cars ever made by Ferrari and it was a completely miserable two days? But I can, and it was.

The following week all hell broke loose. Rumours of 'production issues' at *Top Gear* had been swirling in the tabloids for a while, and suddenly the executive producer Lisa Clark had decided to leave the show. Like everyone else, I just read this stuff in the papers like it had no impact on me. The same happened a few days later when it was revealed that myself and Sabine Schmitz would be presenting the new *Top Gear*. I was in the Tesco car park in Chepstow when friends started messaging me, saying, 'What the hell is this all about?' It was surreal. I was reading about myself in a newspaper.

I didn't enjoy any of it. The actual content of the stories didn't bother me – most of them identified Sabine from the terrific film where she drove Jeremy around the Nürburgring in a Transit – I was just 'unknown bloke who might come from YouTube'. Twenty-four hours passed, some press had got hold of my telephone number and I just hid away with my kids because this was a few days before Christmas. By now it was front-page news everywhere. I waited for the BBC to contact me and tell me what to say – agree or deny, offer a bit of guidance, that kind of thing. But still not a word.

Another day passed and there was still no contact from the BBC. No one had even checked in to ask if everything was okay. I just couldn't understand what was going on. And then my telephone rang with a familiar name on it – James May. 'Hello,' he said 'I'm calling to see if you're okay with everything that's going on, because I'm taking a guess that no one at the BBC has.'

The only person vaguely connected to *Top Gear* who was willing to give me a shoulder to lean on wasn't anyone employed by the corporation, it was a bloke now working on *The Grand Tour* with Jeremy. If anyone tells you that James is anything other than a lovely man, they are lying. I went into Christmas 2015 thinking the world was a very strange place.

Life was grim at that point. I had been 'outed' as working on the new *Top Gear*, so my friends assumed I was now making millions when in fact I was only going to be in half the shows and was making nowhere near that. Easily the best thing that happened in the first quarter of 2016 was meeting Matt LeBlanc at the BBC's sales event in Liverpool. He was kind and fun and, best of all, he clearly loved his cars. He had good knowledge too.

We all had to present a live show to global media buyers, which was fairly cringeworthy. This was the first time the new presenter line-up – me, Sabine, Rory Reid, Eddie Jordan, Matt and Chris Evans – had come together and appeared in one place. I look at the photos now and still can't quite work out what the strategy was, or even if there was a strategy! We were there for two days and Chris Evans didn't really speak to me, so I knew I was already in trouble. But what was I supposed to do – tangle with the man who had complete creative control of *Top Gear*, who was ridiculously famous and powerful? Nah, I just chatted to Matt about 997 GT2s. If in doubt, find a fellow nerd and talk about Porsches. It never fails.

The series was due to air mid-April. I wouldn't be in any of the first four episodes, and my role was quite specific – to cover the track-test stuff on the faster cars. That suited me just fine, but I didn't want to be an outsider and I had serious reservations about the way some of the track tests were written.

This was a big learning curve for me. Online, I came from the fortunate position of knowing my audience well and being certain that there was no limit to how nerdy I could be, or in how much detail we could explore any mechanical element or new technology. *Top Gear* was, and is, completely different: everything had to pass an imaginary idiot test that I found exasperating. The F12tdf film hadn't really exposed me to this because with that car and the old 250 TdF there was a time limit on the film, which meant no one felt the need to dilute it. But when we did a solo film on the then new BMW M2, I was way out of my comfort zone.

This was a single-car shoot, and the writers decided it needed a comic twist to avoid it coming across as a sterile track test. And there was me thinking that's what they'd employed me to do. So instead of describing how the car drove and how it made me feel, they gave me a fictional device to measure how excited my underpants became during cornering. I think it was called the Funometer 3000. Yes, I'm thinking the same as you. But I had to do as I was told.

The first transmission date approached, and we all headed to Dunsfold for the studio recordings. Obviously I had nothing to do whatsoever because I wasn't in the first four episodes, but we did have this weird thing called *Extra Gear*, which was recorded after the main show with myself and Rory. I shared a little dressing room with Rory out the back of the sprawling mass of Portakabins that constitutes the *Top Gear* production office at Dunsfold. It felt like half of the people there had no idea I was even a presenter on the show. I just have that invisible look about me, and most of the time I actually love it. Last year on a job with Pad and Fred one of the people we worked with thought I carried their bags.

The build-up to that first studio record wasn't easy. I had crossed words with Evans a few times and it was abundantly clear that he didn't like me. It was his show and that was fair enough – in my head I was already looking for a new job. Despite this, I had to have faith that what we were doing was going to be good. I desperately wanted it to be, and because I'd loved *Don't Forget Your Toothbrush* and *TFI Friday* as a younger man I just hoped that he would resurrect his live television genius and lift us all – but it didn't happen. I watched that first studio record and thought, 'We're in trouble here.'

The vultures were swirling after that first episode. The *Sun* harried Evans relentlessly, and in my opinion cruelly. The reviews were dire, and not being in those first few shows, which had seemed like a punishment, now felt like something of a blessing. I was immensely lucky that by the time my first sequence aired, in an Aston Martin Vulcan, people decided that a more basic car review of something ostensibly ridiculous with a V12 constituted some automotive comfort food. The reviews were pretty kind, but not remotely glowing.

It was the M2 film a few weeks later that killed me, because it brought home to me what I suspected and most feared might happen if I joined *Top Gear*. My old audience thought I'd sold out. The ones who'd watched me skidding around on YouTube and doing my thing didn't like this mainstream diluted and scripted version of me. And the new television audience went, 'Okay, he can drive a bit, but he's not Jeremy.' For me the outcome couldn't have been worse. Through doing what I was contracted to do on television, I'd managed to alienate the old guard and not impress the new. And as much as I could just about get my head around the criticism, so much of it was incredibly harsh and personal. I was used to some barbs in the YT comments section, but this was another world. I didn't want to leave my flat. I would receive dozens of messages a day saying fairly horrendous things and threatening all sorts too. And all because of a car show. But at least I was earning good money. Oh, no I wasn't. Immediately after the last show aired, Chris Evans announced he was leaving *Top Gear.*

TWENTY-TWO
TG1

We headed off into a summer break not really knowing what was going to happen. The new exec producer Clare Pizey assured me not only that *Top Gear* would resume filming in the autumn, but that I would be a part of it. They even said they'd pay me a bit more money. But not much more.

In late July I headed over to LA to see the Singer boys, but also to meet up with Matt LeBlanc and understand what he thought about *TG* going forwards. This was the first time I'd witnessed a public response to a situation about which I had more facts than most. The papers were saying *TG* was in crisis, when it wasn't at all. In fact, what had happened was the person people found rather challenging had left the building. Where others saw problems, I think we saw some very handy spring-cleaning. Well, it was late summer now, but you know what I mean.

I was quietly over the moon – the person who didn't like me had gone, and the one I got on well with now had a bigger say in what films we made. After a run of poor luck, this seemed like a very jolly outcome indeed.

The first shoot of the new regime was in Montenegro. It was the most beautiful place I'd never heard of before – no wonder the Russians had tried to nick it a few years earlier. The trip out there was a shambles because I had to fly into Croatia and then wait for a taxi that had my name spelt with some additional Zs and Xs. This took a while to untangle, then the taxi had to cross an international border and we went the wrong way for a while and, just for a little bit, I thought something bad might happen to me. That would have stressed me a few years before, but there comes a point where you've had so many strange car journeys that unless you wake up and people are pointing guns at you (Sri Lanka, 2018) then you just go with the flow.

And suddenly life was easy. We'd lanced the boil and *TG* was instantly a much friendlier place. I can remember rolling into the hotel that night and, where six months earlier a few people would have grunted at me and walked away, it was all smiles and laughs – chief among them being Matt.

That was my first big-budget, non-road-test film. There were stunt sequences and huge setup shots and a helicopter and all sorts of other business. There were also many 'pro drivers'. And this was something I found difficult.

The way *Top Gear* used to work is that the presenters would record their pieces talking in the car, wing the wheel around a bit for good entertainment value and then a pro driver would jump into the car and do all the extra shots. In the edit it would all be spliced together to make television. An unfortunate side-effect of this process was that the presenters were made to look better drivers than they actually were. It's the only part of my predecessors' work I ever had any issue with. I didn't want to inherit those work processes, but I did. In fact, I couldn't understand why *TG* hadn't undergone a total reboot when the teams changed, as it seemed like the most logical thing to do. Presenting studio links from that hangar was always odd for me – like sitting in someone else's bathwater. And the pro-driver method remained. At times working on *Top Gear* has been like dealing with someone else's hangover. I had no real creative power.

I've spent the last 25 years learning how to drive. I am not an especially good racing driver, nor am I an especially good rally driver, but if pushed I can turn my hand to both and have a few pots in the basement to prove as much. But there are many people who are miles faster than me and I'm very comfortable with that. I'm also quite good at jumping in pretty much anything and not taking long to understand what its quirks are and how it will behave if you deliberately drive it over the limit. I've ruined a lot of other people's tyres learning how to slide, and I didn't like the fact that *Top Gear* had decided, as I saw it, to hire other talent to make my driving look better. I thought that meant *TG* didn't think my driving was good enough (which I now know wasn't the case). Besides, the skids are the good bit – the idea of wading through all the boring talking-and-filming stuff and then, just when the fun was about to begin, handing over for someone else to have a laugh didn't make any sense.

I thought I'd been hired because I could drive. But there were always other drivers around, to do some of the driving. Montenegro was doubly confusing because for that shoot the lead pro driver and stunt coordinator was my pal Mauro Calo. He's a lovely man and a fine driver, but he also used to do work experience for me back in the *Autocar* days. The *TG* producers were used to the presenters deferring to people like Mauro, but now it had a presenter with more driving experience than many of its professionals.

It took me an embarrassingly long time to understand how to make this work to my advantage, and to not view the presence of the 'professionals' as a threat. Actually, most of them are now my good pals. There was one exception, but he doesn't work there anymore. The final scene we shot in Montenegro involved a police chase and a helicopter and all sorts of madness. Afterwards, a kind chap gave me and Matt a bottle of red wine each. They had our names on the label. All he wanted was a photo of us holding them. We both looked at the labels as he prepared to take his shot – both of us read mine at the same time: 'Chris Evans'. As the photo was taken, Matt grinned and said 'awkward'. I had a good feeling we'd become friends after that.

The next trip was Kazakhstan. This was a triple-header with Matt, myself and Rory. It was to be a celebration of very high-mileage cars – or 'moon-miles' machines as they are sometimes known. We'd take part in some typically silly challenges and then end up at Baikonur – the Russian enclave within Kazakhstan that is home to its space programme. We stayed in the hotel where the Russian and US scientists were working on the International Space Station. This was in 2016 – the world was different back then. Admittedly, even then we were told not to use the Wi-Fi because the Russians had a habit of hacking everyone's computers. The only other absolute rule for that trip was on no account to mention the word 'Borat'. No word of a lie – somewhere in my pile of old documents is a piece of BBC-headed paper informing us that one of the conditions of being granted a visa for filming was not ever saying the word 'Borat' or even referring to the character. *Jagshemash!*

That trip was memorable for good and bad reasons. The list of good things was very long. Despite the astonishing cold, and hotels far rougher than anything I've seen in Africa, we had some outrageous experiences. I spent an afternoon driving up and down the longest runway I've ever seen, which was built to land the Buran, the former Soviet Union's space shuttle. They have one of the three surviving Burans at the cosmodrome museum nearby and you can sit in the cockpit. It's slowly rotting outside, along with the odd rocket motor. It's a magnificent place I fear westerners might someday soon be banned from visiting. I still have my Baikonur bottle opener and notepad.

We also saw a Soyuz rocket launch from about 1.5km away – that was the end shot to the film. To all of those lucky enough to have witnessed one of these events, I'm sure you feel equally unable to describe it in words. Seven years later I still cannot understand how a man-made object is capable of rattling internal organs from a mile away. It's one of those experiences that I would never have put anywhere near my bucket list, but now I've seen it I have to admit it should have been at the very top. It's a logical outcome too – I love man-made things that produce power and go fast, and a rocket designed to power its way out of Earth's atmosphere is the ultimate expression of those passions. Luckily it was an unmanned mission because it blew up not long after we last saw it. That bit didn't make the edit.

Later, we had a local tribe persuade us to eat a cooked sheep's head that was on the turn, and watched a version of polo that used a goat torso instead of a ball. For a while it was like being on the set of *Game of Thrones*. There's a separate book for 'scenes that looked too bonkers in the edit'. We also had a race in our cars down into a quarry – and that's where the bad thing happened.

Towards the end of the race, myself and Rory were bearing down on Matt in his ageing German taxi. The closing speed was big. I was side-by-side with Rory in his taxi and I needed to jink right to not pile into the back of the most famous man I'd ever met. Probably still have ever met. I didn't get the room I needed and hit the back of the Mercedes very, very hard. Luckily, Matt is a very well-built guy – if he wasn't I think he could have been in serious trouble. The onboard footage is pretty shocking. It happened so quickly, all I could think was, 'Shit, I just killed Joey.'

The practical fallout from the incident wasn't helpful – it was day one of the shoot and my Volvo's front was badly mangled. Without *TG*'s mechanical fixing guru Peter Ross, it would have gone straight in the bin. But there aren't many Volvo V70s in Kazakhstan, especially with the rare Audi five-cylinder engine. So it was patched up.

My head wasn't, though. When you film cars you have to be able to trust what the other people are going to do in them, and I trusted Matt, and ended up spending more and more time filming with him. Which I really enjoyed. And the numbers were growing again. The uncomfortable truth is that during the eight episodes Chris Evans presented we shipped viewers like a holed supertanker. The first episode was watched by well over six million people, the last by under two million. I'm no great student of the numbers, but I can't think of many shows that have lost so many viewers in such a short time. We were having to rebuild against a prevailing trend of falling audience numbers across the linear television landscape. Not an easy job, but it was happening.

Also, the perennial negativity was something I never want to experience again. For a while, and from where I was sitting, everyone just wanted us to fail. I now realise that wasn't the case, but when you wake up to several thousand messages on Twitter saying how shit you are at your job, no matter how tough you may think you are, it's soul-destroying.

In the space of a year I'd gone from being the fresh-faced independent chap who battled the forces of YouTube, to delivering – for FREE – the great Holy Trinity supercar test of our times, to the bloke on *Top Gear* who wasn't very good. Even though I loved working with Matt, this change in status was something I didn't anticipate being so harsh – which is shame-fully naive. Why was I so blindsided by this, given that I'd written about the pitfalls of taking the job? I was seduced by being offered access to something I could only have dreamt about, and part of that fairy-tale process inevitably involves a dose of denial.

The closest car nerds can come to understanding how this feels is realising the dream of owning the poster car of your youth. Imagine it was a Ferrari Testarossa – you've spent 30 years dreaming about that machine when, through hard work, you find yourself in the position to buy one. On the drive home you squirm around in the uncomfortable driver's seat and wonder why the air-conditioning is so bad and the gearshift is a bit tricky. And when you finally get the chance to wang that flat 12-cylinder motor – the one you'd always assumed you'd never even hear, let alone control – a BMW M140i saunters past like you're stationary. It dawns on you that the reality is nothing like the dream. That was *Top Gear* at the start. I was now recognisable to the man on the street (not the woman) but wasn't being remunerated the way people might have expected.

Our reaction to those situations is never straightforward. To continue the car analogy, do you park the unavoidable objective observations and decide to enjoy the machine for what it represents? Your achievement in just being able to afford it? The beauty of its bodywork? More tellingly, do you share how you feel about it to those close to you? Climbing into the car at a pub as a passing stranger says, 'Beautiful car,' your inner voice might want to reply, 'It's beautiful, but it drives with all the sophistication of a rusty rotavator.' But if you say that out loud, do you not only shatter your own illusion of that car and your own achievements, but that other person's view of a beautiful Ferrari? No one should want to be the purveyor of misery.

That was the awful truth about *Top Gear*. During that first year, complete strangers would quite understandably come barrelling up and say, 'You've got the best job in world!' And I'd smile and say, 'Yeah, it's amazing! I'm so lucky!' But I was lying. At any point in 2016 I would have swapped this terrifying new reality of bile and Twitter hatred for being the surprisingly-enjoyable-to-watch bloke on YouTube once again. Imagine the shattering disappointment on the face of a young kid who loves *Top Gear* and heard one of the lucky bastards who gets to skid all those cars around saying it was actually a pain in the arse? It's unacceptable behaviour, right up there with telling a six-year-old the man with the white beard doesn't wriggle down the chimney each Christmas. For a long time, presenting *Top Gear* and not being Jeremy sucked. That changed over time, but the beginning was crap.

Much of the polarised response was completely irrational, too. I reviewed an Alfa Giulia Quadrifoglio for the TV show and received the usual barrage of abuse, but when we posted an inferior film on YouTube people loved it! A large part of the UK audience had decided that whatever we did on the new *Top Gear* was shit before they'd even watched it. At the peak of my pained paranoia I can remember sitting and watching Twitter as an episode aired at 8pm one Sunday. By 8.01pm there were hundreds of people saying, 'This is so shit.' The opening credits hadn't even finished. I'll put my hands up and admit that we struggled to match the previous three when they were at their best, but we made some films I'm still very proud of. And Matt? Go and watch the film he made with the late, great Ken Block – it's an absolute belter. One of the best things ever released under the *Top Gear* banner, and yet the entire Chris Evans era is dismissed as being shit.

I didn't read reviews of the show because after the Evans series that was a one-way ticket to therapy. But one day something was sent to me, or I read it in a magazine – I can't remember which. It was the most coruscating deconstruction of my professional life I could ever have imagined reading. The type of thing you'd shield your children from seeing. It was in *GQ* magazine, and the reason it hit me so hard was that it was so well written. The writer was someone called Rupert Myers. I should really quote chunks of it so you can marvel at the way he applied the scalpel to my limited talents. The writing reeked of the joy he took from pointing out how bad I was, and it was of very high quality. That was a new one – I was used to the angry Twitter 'you're not Jeremy' outburst, but here was a grinning, capable assassin. I must have been crying and laughing simultaneously because I will always appreciate writing of that quality, no matter if it makes me drink a bottle of single malt and hide from the world for two days. I mention that article because soon after that Rupert Myers landed in some trouble due to his treatment of women and his media career ended overnight. He eventually wrote about the effect his fall from grace had on his mental health and career. I read some of it and didn't know how to process his predicament. What he wrote about me tipped me into a bad place for a while, and now he was looking for sympathy for his own mental health through some kind of mea culpa. The media really is a strange place. As you can imagine, I haven't read a review since then.

I cannot understand why anyone would want to be famous. The two most valuable commodities in life are time and privacy. Interacting with people who recognise you off the back of being on television is something I'm not very good at – I try to be polite and give everyone some time, but I have no doubt my shoulders are stiff with awkwardness and insecurity. Like many people who end up on telly, I'm a shy extrovert. In my comfort zone I'm the Japanese knotweed of the conversation – an ever-present menace you'd rather be rid of. Away from that place I'm awkward and quiet and don't want to talk to people.

One side of *Top Gear* has always protected me, though – I have always worked with people far more famous than me. Nothing could suit me more perfectly than walking into a room with a co-presenter and being instantly invisible. I've seen other people on *Top Gear* struggle with fighting for the limelight, but if you're sitting at a round-table press event with Matt LeBlanc I'm afraid you either have to be comfortable with no one being remotely interested in you or grind up against the wall in a pink mankini to garner some attention.

CHAPTER TWENTY-TWO

All of them – Matt, Paddy and Fred – have acted as a lightning rod for me. I suppose it harks back to boarding school and my job at *Autocar* – I like there being a boss, a bigger dog, and I'll slot in behind and follow. For the rest of 2016 and into 2017 that's what I did with Matt. Filming became fun again, and I'd look forward to going away. The best trip was to Northern California so Matt could indulge his passion for the legend of Bigfoot. This was peak *Top Gear* for me – cars, bikes, crazy off-roaders, and a flying ATV called the SkyRunner (I'd describe it as an off-road buggy with a parachute). I'm often asked what the silliest thing I've done on *Top Gear* is, and despite the fact we took off, flew about and landed without too many issues, that might be it. Waiting at the airport to fly home, I was grazing YouTube and found a video of a SkyRunner flying around – and straight into a building. The footage was horrific. That was probably the first time I thought that I should maybe think a little longer and harder before just throwing myself at mechanical objects.

TWENTY-THREE
TG2

While I was making *Top Gear* I was still able to film the NBC show called *DRIVE* with JF and my old YouTube family. Television is riddled with inertia and problems. People who drop in on that world cannot believe how long things take. The NBC films were much less involved, and that was the perfect antidote to *TG*. In 2016 we were still trying to sell DRIVE. In fact Emil, who I hadn't spoken to in ages, managed to reach heads-of-terms on a deal to sell the brand and the back catalogue to Time Inc. Fair play to him – I assumed DRIVE was dead and worthless, but he persevered.

The only slight fly in the ointment was that as he pushed that deal over the line, the FBI decided it wanted to chat to him about a fraud at Epix, where Emil worked. I was filming the new Honda NSX at Monticello in New York when JF called: 'You won't believe this – Emil has been arrested for fraud.'

Quite a big fraud as it turned out – nearly $8 million taken from his employer at Epix. Initially I just giggled, because that's what you do when presented with such a delicious dose of schadenfreude. Then my brain fizzed off into more worrying territory. I seemed to recall something in the BBC contract about being associated with criminal activities, etc., and was worried. I am the bloke that always ends up in the shit for some reason, often for being the idiot in the wrong place at the wrong time.

The FBI interviewed JF, which must rank highly as a non-bucket-list activity, but they never came knocking for me. The problem is, once the FBI was involved the transaction had to be paused and I had been rather looking forward to that little chunk of money. The deal did go through, and the BBC never knew anything about it, but the proceeds took ages to land. Because I'm financially prudent, I invested much of it into a 12-year-old 70,000-mile Rolls-Royce Phantom, which promptly shat its steering column and two fuel pumps, generating a nice little £12,000 bill. Oh, and Emil went to jail for four years.

I loved that Phantom. It lived with us for a year, and we played the *Jungle Book* soundtrack non-stop and treated it like a Vauxhall Zafira. At the British GP the next summer I parked it next to a Ferrari 355, out of which a very large man was trying to emerge. It was Frank Bruno – somewhere I have a selfie with Frank and the Rolls. As you can probably tell by the complete lack of celeb stories in this book, I'm not really interested in that life and keep away. But Frank Bruno can melt your heart in 30 seconds. That sodding Roller could then break it in half. Most expensive car I've ever owned, unsurprisingly.

At the end of 2017, Rory's role on *Top Gear* changed, so it was just myself and Matt presenting non-studio films. The template was for three presenters, but two seemed to work just fine, so we set off for Sri Lanka to make a film celebrating the humble tuk-tuk. It was the standard *TG* adventure with all manner of things going wrong. Notwithstanding the guns – I was asleep heading back from the Tamil north when we woke up at an especially spicy checkpoint where people were pointing guns at each other. We Brits always find them quite shocking.

Sri Lanka was notable for two reasons, both of them being editorial. The vast majority of what you see on *Top Gear* actually happens – the situations in which they happen may have been constructed to facilitate that mishap, or story thread, but the cameras roll and capture what they capture.

Just occasionally, we might need to amplify something to add some excitement, or it might just be that the story arc expected something to happen to a vehicle but it stubbornly refused to play ball. Enter the tuk-tuk that would not roll onto its side.

Anyone who has ever driven one of these little death-traps will confirm that even when stationary, they feel like they might just flop onto their side – like a Labrador next to an open fire. Loaded to the gunnels with bag of tea leaves, it should have been willing to roll at any speed, but by some quirk of physics it didn't want to play flip-flop, so we set about trying to make it happen. Enter Niall McShea, ex-rally driver and fearless pro driver on *Top Gear*. Niall was charged with plonking said three-wheeler onto its side and, for the first attempt, fired it through a tight corner far faster than anyone would normally dare. Nothing but understeer. He was giggling, I was wedged in between bags of tea in the back, laughing even more. I had so much PG Tips as padding, I couldn't have been safer. We tried again, faster this time. Still the bloody thing wouldn't tip – excuse the pun. For the third and final attempt Niall made sure that we were going over. This time the machine obeyed, fell flat on its side and all I could hear was laughter.

And this is when *Top Gear* is the best job in the world, when the director and the producer and the runners and researchers and the hosts and the camera operators and the soundies are all doubled over giggling. Maybe I realised we had been missing that during my first couple of years on *TG*, but it landed that day. Yes, I was always laughing with Matt offscreen, but this time it felt more powerful.

A few days later we were up in the very north of the country, attempting to sail the tuk-tuks, which now wore inflatable outriggers, to India. As you do. For this scene my tuk-tuk needed to sink, which it would have done anyway, but let's just say that for the benefit of the crew and presenters we might have added a little assistance to the sinking process. She went down rather faster than expected, which posed a few difficulties for me because the whole vessel became a mess of rope and sharp metal into which I was tangled. There's one photo where my head is a little too low in the water for comfort.

Anyhow, the extraction isn't the reason for telling you this. The drone shot covering all the action is. No one had told us about the shark tracking all this. The man filming it all, torso-deep in water next to the sinking tuk-tuk, was Iain May, a kind of Swiss-army cameraman without whom I'm not sure *Top Gear* could even exist. I'll happily sink and swim, but I'm not into being tracked by a shark.

A few months later Matt decided to leave *Top Gear*. He'd effectively been commuting between LA and the UK, and, as anyone who has attempted that will understand, it leaves your body fighting a constant fug of jetlag. He phoned me just as I was about to drive the fastest car I've ever driven, the Porsche 919, to tell me he was going. If I look a little preoccupied in that film, you now know why. It was a logical decision for him, and I had no idea how the BBC would react.

There were a couple of months to take stock. Furthermore, I had taken delivery of a 991 GT3 Touring, my first new special Porsche, so life was pretty good. Because I'd been working hard on *TG* and other projects for some time, I wasn't necessarily aware how comfortable I'd become on *Top Gear*. I loved working with Matt and his little team of people, the show's numbers were good, the BBC was happy, and I had my dream 911. Without realising it, life had become great. And now it required a reboot – again.

Of those six people photographed in January 2016, and revealed as the new hosts of *Top Gear*, I was the last one standing. This was only two years later. Not many people would have betted on that outcome, least of all me. I suppose it's a badge of honour in some way. Or maybe I'm so loath-some they all ran away? The BBC said it had every intention of continuing with the show and so the process of choosing two new co-hosts would begin. The net was cast as wide as possible, and we set about the process.

This supposedly meant a summer of leisure, but that never happens, and I was filling my time doing as much racing as possible. The main events were the Blancpain GT3 races with the Garage 59 team. For 2018 we had an Aston Martin Vantage whose rear axle I could never really make work prop-erly. The Spa 24hrs is the season peak for all the teams, but I've never finished that bastard of an event, let alone enjoyed it. However, the four-hour race at Paul Ricard was always a highlight. The sun always shone, we always did well and sometimes Alex would fly us back on a plane that didn't have any writing on it. I felt like a very lucky boy. Actually, despite all my demons, I've always felt lucky – if you have no idea where you came from and your reality involves racing cars and *Top Gear*, you probably should.

One day that summer I decided to go and watch the cricket at Edgbaston. Parking was a nightmare, so I plonked the 911 halfway up a grass verge in some residential area (you can do that in a Porsche, but not a Ferrari) and then wandered off to find a ticket. My phone rang – it was Edward Lovett. We'd always stayed in contact sporadically. He told me he wanted to build and launch an online auction site for cars in the UK. Anything to do with buying and selling cars interests me. Throughout my freelance years I would always top up my writing income with some car trading. It was useful money, but also kept me in contact with all manner of amusing human beings. There is more comedy content in the motor trade than anywhere else I know.

And I've always loved car classifieds – over time they'd become my default editorial content – so the idea of a curated online auction platform excited me. If anyone else typed that it would be a paid-for lie, but I hope you're now getting an idea that these sorts of things float my boat. Plus, an American equivalent to this had been rumbling along for some time and was gaining significant traction. Edward asked if I wanted to be involved – of course I did. And, technically, I didn't have a BBC contract, so I was free to engage with whomever I wanted.

In August we ran screen tests for the new roles on *Top Gear*. The process of selecting those people was quite straightforward – once you eliminate everyone who isn't available or wouldn't touch it with a barge pole, and be realistic about who could competently deliver the role required of them, the pool of people is surprisingly small. You now know the outcome of those tests.

I suppose there were only two people that I ever regretted not persuading to do *Top Gear*, and that's not because they would have taken such a job – they clearly wouldn't – but because I think we've only seen brief glimpses of their genius in the context of reviewing cars, and as serial car magazine/film/television nerds. They were Steve Coogan and Rowan Atkinson. We couldn't have afforded one limb of either, but they are clearly people obsessed with cars and who have an ability to place them in perfect context. But it was never going to happen – and maybe I've written that as a response to all the people who have asked me what my dream *TG* line-up would be. For the avoidance of doubt, in that imaginary world, I wouldn't be the third presenter.

The screen tests were incredibly straightforward. If you'd said to me a month earlier that Paddy McGuinness and Andrew Flintoff would be complete shoo-ins for the roles, of course I wouldn't have believed you. But beyond their obvious presenting skills you need to be aware of two things. Firstly, they both arrived in proper cars: Paddy a BMW 1M and Fred a Ferrari FF. Albeit on chav aftermarket wheels, something we have chuckled about many times since. The other is that for quite different reasons I wanted to love both of them, because I'm a cricket tragic and I think *Phoenix Nights* is one of the funniest shows ever committed to film. If you want to like people, they will probably like you back. The decision to hire them was made very quickly, and the announcement came way sooner than expected.

The usual negative abuse was of course expected, and as per the previous few years *Top Gear* was dead and too white (personally I found that one tricky!) and too middle-aged. And you know what? None of it mattered because I was battle hardened to all the peripheral crap now and just wanted to get on with filming. It was always going to be fun.

The first shoot was nearly our last shoot. Paddy converted a hearse into the ultimate family car, which made for many amusing scenes, including one where we demonstrated the car's ability to fire down a rally stage. The only problem here was that it wasn't a rally car and it rolled. Hearses aren't designed to roll, and I can now advise anyone attempting to roll one that it's not a good idea. Despite a bent neck and a sore back, I knew we were in good shape after that film. Both of them were fantastic fun, and even though it would take a little time for the dynamic to settle down and each player to find their role in the team, I was blessed with two funny blokes who wanted to get stuck in. From the start we laughed constantly, and nothing was off the table when it came to piss-taking, including me having a massive crash, outside of filming, in my beloved 911 because some dopey prick attempted to do a three-point turn on a blind bend.

'Are you alive?' asked Pad when he saw news of the crash.

'Yes,' I replied.

'Shame.'

The first season with Pad and Fred aired in 2019, the reviews (I'm told) were pretty good, and the audience grew. Of all the reboots I've been involved in, this was the smoothest. I doubt I'll ever have a more intense filming year than 2019 – my passport shows big productions in Ethiopia, Nepal and Peru, and a heap of European travel too.

They may look and sound like they come from a similar place, but there is one profound difference between the two: Fred has travelled to most corners of the globe and could live in a tree, unconnected to civilization, whereas Pad, certainly at the start of his *TG* journey, needed to be within a mile of a KFC or he felt unsettled. Watching him move from being utterly horrified as I ate a very moody lamb curry in Ethiopia to being the man who would casually say, 'Have you tried the dahl?' is to witness the journey of a boy into adulthood. Admittedly, a year later when he watched me eat a ram's testicle he did retch quite severely.

What I remember most is the laughter. There's some friction now and again but it never lasts that long, and sitting here I'm just smiling at the instances when people were reduced to tears. If I believe that time and privacy are the most valuable human commodities, then laughter is the emotional drug that we should all allow ourselves to be become addicted to. If you spend your days laughing as you work, it's hardly a job. I suppose my only note of caution is that at times I've felt that not enough of that laughter made it into the finished television show, but that's not under my control.

Being someone who was a little fed up with international travel in January 2020 will now be viewed as a serious miscalculation. But I was. Covid came out of nowhere, and before we knew it life changed. As someone who hasn't really been located anywhere with any permanence since, well, he was born, it came as a huge shock. There's a reason why, a few months into the lockdown, I was posting nightly Instagram stories called 'The Whisky Files' and sporting a bleached white Mohican. I don't remember recording a single one of those now, and I ended up in a pickle that summer. The people who helped me out of it know who they are, and how much I love them for the help.

I think we all emerged from the lockdown full of trepidation and fear. Many of the permanent social and economic fractures of our lives had disappeared, swept away by a virus. But *Top Gear* continued – in fact, we were given dispensation to start filming a series during the lockdown as part of a 'get Britain back to normal again' strategy formed by the BBC. We did that by going to Alton Towers and filming while it was deserted. An odd way to present some normality to people.

The relationship between the three of us was so relaxed that the films became easier. The production team worked like dogs as usual, and of course we all put in the hours as presented, but there was now an underlying security that so long as some vaguely interesting material was available we'd be fine. That still meant we'd be lobbed at some fairly uncomfortable challenges, chief among them being the wall of death – that was the worst challenge I've done for *Top Gear*, but not for the reason you might expect.

Driving around a vertical wall at 60mph is about as unpleasant as you'd think. The car bumping around so severely you can't really see what you're doing begins an unpleasant process, but as the G-forces pull the blood away from your head and into your feet, you try and tense your core to keep it from happening. Which leaves you looking like you are doing a large poo.

With your poo-face being recorded for the nation, you now begin to grey-out a bit and a wave of the dangerous euphoria we all experience just before blacking out washes over you. Then the car gently falls back down to the centre.

CHAPTER TWENTY-THREE

The problem? None of this translated into tense television. At the time if you'd asked us what was the worst thing we'd done on *Top Gear* we would have each answered 'the wall of death'. There is no right and wrong in that situation and there certainly isn't a rule book for making great films – but the one situation you really should avoid is doing something genuinely riddled with danger and jeopardy that just doesn't work when broadcast.

AFTERWORD
THE FUTURE

I'm sitting here now in September 2023, and I haven't made a *Top Gear* film for ten months. In December 2022 Fred had an accident while filming at Dunsfold. I was there that day and the only thing I want to say on the subject is that I'm happy he's still with us. I don't make friends easily, but Fred and Pad have been kind to me and I love them an awful lot. I miss working with them.

My world has fallen apart a little bit, but I'm ready for another reboot. Why not? I've managed a few before, and there should be enough left in the tank for one more. I really don't know what the future holds right now – it could be *Top Gear*, it could be something quite different. That doesn't scare me, it's just the way life has always been.

And, of course, I have a whole life outside of this car nonsense that you have all correctly assumed I don't share with people. Imagine writing a book and not mentioning the three most important things in your life – your brilliant, beautiful and eternally challenging children. Imagine not mentioning the old friendships that have supplanted the wider family I never had; the half-brother I call a brother, who must have viewed all of this weirdness with an even greater sense of bewilderment than even my parents. It's felt very odd doing that at times, but I just don't go there. Why anyone would share their private life with strangers on social media platforms is a question I'll never be able to answer. My weird life belongs to me and those closest to me. It's baffling that anyone would be remotely interested in any of it. My children are cleverer and better than me, and I hope they'll make better decisions. And if they make bad ones, who cares? All of it is fixable.

That conversation in 2018 with Edward Lovett turned into a business called Collecting Cars. It's now the biggest online automotive auction house in the UK and I'm very proud of what we've achieved. I've just started making some YouTube films again, and it feels good. An early-nineties polit-ician would observe that life is now, finally, offering some 'green shoots'.

At the centre of it all is, and always has been, the motor car. Now a pariah and an object of hate for many, I remain unashamedly in love with them. They are the only constant throughout this book, and in my life to date. Five minutes from now, I'll be in my 911, and all will be good with the world.

INDEX